More Advance Praise for *It's Your Biz*

"Susan Solovic has written a needed book that offers prospective business owners both a realistic view of the hurdles they'll face and powerful strategies for tackling them. Read it for a confidence boost that will help you build your business and yourself."

—Mark Sanborn, author of *The Fred Factor* and
You Don't Need a Title to Be a Leader

"In the middle of my life, I left a long career in journalism to launch a business from scratch. I wish I'd read *It's Your Biz* first, because it would have saved me a lot of time and money. Susan Solovic is absolutely right that being an entrepreneur—romantic as it sounds—isn't for everyone. She lays out a very clear, compelling guide to figuring out whether running your own business is the right move for you."

—Tony Schwartz, author of *New York Times* bestseller
Be Excellent at Anything and *Power of Full Engagement*

"About to pour your time and money into starting the business of your dreams? There's more to it than you might think, but Solovic has a few tricks up her sleeve that you'll put to good use. *It's Your Biz* will help you look before you leap!"

Charlene Li, Founder of Altimeter Group and
author of *Open Leadership* and *Groundswell*

"The only person that can give advice on how to start and grow a business is a person who has done it herself, and Susan Solovic is that person. In her book *It's Your Biz*, she shares all that she's learned—the good, the bad and the ugly—and tells us how to move into action. Whether you are a first-time entrepreneur or are repositioning your business after a rough recession, *It's Your Biz* will give you the insights, action items, and tips you need to make sure that you take control of your business into the future. Business owners will reap great rewards from reading this easy-to-read business 'how to' book!"

—Leslie Grossman, Cofounder, Women's Leadership Exchange

"It's simple. If you are starting a business or struggling with an existing one, you need this book. Filled with tips, ideas, and strategies, it is your roadmap to success."

—Shep Hyken, *New York Times* bestselling
author of *The Amazement Revolution*

"*It's Your Biz* is filled with tons of practical advice and pearls of wisdom on how to turn your passion into a profitable, sustainable business."

—Jill Konrath, author of *SNAP Selling* and *Selling to Big Companies*

"It's become common wisdom that the best way to succeed in any endeavor is to seek out someone who has already succeeded in doing what you want to do and duplicate their methods. Meet your new mentor, Susan Solovic. She is the real deal, a proven entity who has built successful businesses. Reading this book is like sitting at the feet of a master. Read, learn, prosper!"

—Bob Burg, coauthor of *The Go-Giver* and *Endless Referrals*

"I met Susan Solovic in 2005 when she was booked as a guest on ABC's *World News This Morning*. As the overnight and early morning news anchor at ABC News I had interviewed numerous 'experts' from all walks of business life. As Susan became a regular on the morning news I found her to be the most passionate and point blank of any our guests. She preached the gospel of small business in such a way that anyone with an idea or inkling to start a business couldn't help but give it serious consideration. But unlike scores of others who claim a place in the world of small-business entrepreneurship, Susan always kept it real. She shed a light on the challenges small-business owners face, and offered a range of solutions.

"There are many small-business 'experts' who can inspire you to try something new—leave you feeling as if you can do anything. But being able to navigate the sometimes difficult road that is small business takes an expert of a different kind. This book will undoubtedly awaken your entrepreneurial spirit—Susan will surely motivate, inspire, and enlighten. BUT, she will make sure you're never blindsided by the real-life challenges and problems that are sure to arise.

"I know it sounds cliché, but it is a fitting analogy—success is a marathon, not a sprint. Susan will fire the starting pistol and see you off on the race. Then she will show up by your side to coach you through the most difficult stretch, when you're running out of breath and your legs are giving out. She will help get you to that place where the finish line is in sight. The time is now to get in the race, but don't go it alone."

—Ron Corning, WFAA-TV Morning Anchor, Dallas, Texas

IT'S YOUR BIZ

it's your biz

the complete guide to becoming your own boss

SUSAN WILSON SOLOVIC
WITH ELLEN R. KADIN

FOREWORD BY EDIE WEINER

AMACOM AMERICAN MANAGEMENT ASSOCIATION
New York • Atlanta • Brussels • Chicago • Mexico City
San Francisco • Shanghai • Tokyo • Toronto • Washington, D.C.

Bulk discounts available. For details visit:
www.amacombooks.org/go/specialsales
Or contact special sales: Phone: 800-250-5308 / Email: specialsls@amanet.org
View all the AMACOM titles at: www.amacombooks.org

This publication is designed to provide accurate and authoritative information in regard to the subject matter covered. It is sold with the understanding that the publisher is not engaged in rendering legal, accounting, or other professional service. If legal advice or other expert assistance is required, the services of a competent professional person should be sought.

Although this book does not always specifically identify trademarked terms, AMACOM uses them for editorial purposes only, with no intention of trademark violation.

"It's Your Biz" is a trademark of Susan Solovic Media.

"Saving People Money So They Can Live Better" is a registered service mark of Wal-Mart Stores, Inc.

Library of Congress Cataloging-in-Publication Data

Solovic, Susan Wilson.
    It's your biz : the complete guide to becoming your own boss / Susan Wilson Solovic, with Ellen R. Kadin ; foreword by Edie Weiner.
       p. cm.
    Includes bibliographical references and index.
    ISBN-13: 978-0-8144-1671-6 (hbk.)
    ISBN-10: 0-8144-1671-3 (hbk.)
    1. New business enterprises. 2. Business planning. 3. Small business—Management.
I. Kadin, Ellen R. II. Title.
    HD62.5.S6729 2012
    658.1'1—dc23

                                               2011017507

About AMA

American Management Association (www.amanet.org) is a world leader in talent development, advancing the skills of individuals to drive business success. Our mission is to support the goals of individuals and organizations through a complete range of products and services, including classroom and virtual seminars, webcasts, webinars, podcasts, conferences, corporate and government solutions, business books, and research. AMA's approach to improving performance combines experiential learning—learning through doing—with opportunities for ongoing professional growth at every step of one's career journey.

Printing number
10 9 8 7 6 5 4 3 2 1

To my loving husband, George, who is my biggest fan, best friend, and source of inspiration. We love each other unconditionally. I could never have achieved so much without his loving support.

■ ■ ■

To my stepgrandchildren: Brendan, Emma, Matthew, and Claire. I hope in some small way I help you to see the world as a source of inspiration, and I hope you find the courage to discover your special talents, to be confident enough to follow your passions, and to use your talents to make your mark on the world.

—Susan Wilson Solovic

CONTENTS

FOREWORD

I have often credited ignorance with the starting and building of my business in 1977. I believe that if I had known what I was getting into, I would never have done it in the first place. But that is not a prescription for success, only for taking the risk. I probably could have gotten a lot further, and a lot faster, if this book had been available 34 years ago.

In the intervening years, I have seen friends, family, and acquaintances start businesses by the dozens. Some of them took the entrepreneurial path because they truly wanted to. Others were pressed into it as a result of layoffs, forced retirement, or burnout. Most limped along in their fledgling enterprises, and many failed. None of this was due to a lack of commitment, vision, or hard work. More often, it was because of a lack of good advice, poor planning, and a weak support network.

I am so happy that Susan and Ellen have written this book as a bible for all those entrepreneurs-in-waiting. We are going through a fundamental economic restructuring, and it is global and it is permanent. As futurists, we have seen this restructuring coming and have been following its consequences closely. Productivity goes up as real wages and expansive employment in the industrial world go down. On top of that, the industrial world is aging, with millions of people over 65 looking for relevance, as well as income, to sustain the last decades of their lives. Being able to get a well-paying job at any age that is both satisfying and secure is no longer the norm but, rather, the exception. Not everyone is born an entrepreneur, but many will want to learn how to become one. We will need many more tools to help people learn to do it right. This book is an important and needed addition to that tool kit.

We all approach reaching our goals differently. Some drive for financial success without thinking of the greater community. Some care about the public good and neglect the business fundamentals. Increasingly, we see budding entrepreneurs comparing themselves to the Internet billionaires, or the social entrepreneurs who have changed the public landscape. Whatever your goals, the business basics are the same. Without sound underpinnings, your goals will elude you, and your work will be for naught. If you are contemplating starting any kind of business, for whatever purposes you lay out in front of you, remember that it is still a business. You are not gambling against the house, you are not hoping to win the lottery, and you are not volunteering. You are starting a business. And the business of business is business.

Read this book. Use this book. Your future and the future of the world are bound together by the innovation and creativity we collectively bring to the work we do. Make that work count, and make it successfully endure. Ensure that your business endures, and make this book work for you.

—Edie Weiner, Futurist
President, Weiner, Edrich, Brown, Inc.

introduction

WHY AM I writing this book? Because you need it. That may sound arrogant, but it's true. I've spent decades learning—sometimes the hard way—what really makes small businesses work. I started my first business when I was 15 years old, and I have always been intrigued by the myriad opportunities there are to use your own resources to make money.

I've been a serial entrepreneur. Not that everything I've done has been a success, but fortunately I've had more successes than failures.

And while it is always nice to bask in the glow of my successes, I've definitely learned more from my missteps.

I've also spoken with countless entrepreneurs around the world, hearing about and learning from their problems and stories. I've delivered keynote speeches and seminars to hundreds of thousands of people with small businesses, and I have listened to their feedback. I've taught college-level entrepreneurship courses, and many of my students have gone on to build successful companies. And as a journalist, I've covered countless business conferences and have reported on a plethora of topics related to operating a small business in this country. As a media expert on small-business operations, I've taken on hundreds of topics and answered hundreds of viewer questions. Suffice it to say, I've seen, heard, and experienced a lot, whether directly or through others. My goal in this book is to leverage that experience to save you time, effort, resources, and aggravation as you start up your own business.

■ ■ ■

In the pages that follow, I give you the realities of what it takes to start and grow a *successful* small business—especially in today's economic environment. There are millions of people starting businesses all the time, and millions more who are dreaming about becoming their own boss. All of them have talents, skills, and ideas; but without understanding certain fundamental business principles, their chances of being among the failed-business-venture statistics are high.

Yes, there are exceptions to every rule, and I acknowledge that sometimes someone simply gets lucky in business; but most entrepreneurs have to work extremely hard. And part of that hard work is seeing past the romantic vision of launching your small business and focusing on the cold, hard reality of what it takes to build a business. The bottom line is: *What you don't know will hurt you.*

The recent recession has transformed the long-established business paradigm more dramatically than at any other time since perhaps the Industrial Revolution, which turned traditional employment on its ear. I submit that we are entering a new era in which the majority of Americans will either own a small business or work for one. Large companies will always exist, but not on the grand pre-recession scale. Having learned to do more with less, many big firms will outsource work when it is needed. And who will do that work? It could be you, as an independent worker or operating your own small business.

· · ·

Allow me to put this in perspective. Back in 2003, there were massive downsizings, and many of my friends and family members for the first time in their lives joined the ranks of the unemployed. They were traumatized by pink slips and the reality that there was no longer a place for them in the company where they had spent the majority of their professional lives. Shell-shocked by the abrupt change in their lives, they were lost and afraid, their self-esteem shaken to the core. "Who am I without my job?" they asked.

I watched people's lives be nearly destroyed after they had been discarded by their companies, and I felt a strong desire to help. I wanted to inspire them, to help them see themselves as much more than a job title followed by a company name. These were talented, unique individuals, and I wanted to encourage them to look at their unique and special gifts—to focus on the very real difference between having a job-related skill and having inherent talents. Why? Because it's our special talents—the things we are really, really good at—that are the essence of who we are. Tapping into these special talents can help you make a smooth transition from one career path to another. In other words, your unique gifts give you the ability to reinvent yourself, and likewise, to reinvent your professional career.

So, in 2003, I wrote a book called *Reinvent Your Career: Obtain the Success You Desire and Deserve.* In this book, I described an interview with a woman who had been a professional flutist and reinvented herself to become a genetic researcher. Seems a far reach, doesn't it? But not when you recognize, as she did, that music, like research, is based on mathematics. Her mathematic skills enabled her to transition easily to a new and more lucrative career.

Since I wrote that book, the business world has evolved even more. The recent economic recession has wrought millions of unemployed workers, an unprecedented number of home foreclosures, countless major retail brands boarded up for good, a rash of business and personal bankruptcies, and an unstable financial market. Even as the economy rebounds, there simply won't be enough jobs available to absorb all those millions of unemployed and displaced American workers. At many companies, streamlined operations have reduced staffing needs. And increasingly sophisticated technology continues to replace many job functions, further reducing the need for human capital.

Millions of Americans are facing the stark reality that they need to rely on themselves—and their own resources—in order to provide for their economic well-being. Stealing a phrase from the '70s era, "There's no trust in working for the man." People are fed up with working crazy, long hours for a bureaucratic entity, sacrificing balance in their personal lives and their well-being in order to line someone else's pockets.

In this new business paradigm, it's no longer about reinventing your career or looking for creative ways to rev up your job search. Today, it's about building your career as a freelancer, an independent contractor, consultant, small-business owner, or franchisee. Now is the time to focus on what it is you can create and deliver to the market.

. . .

Whether you leave the employment ranks voluntarily or involuntarily, the landscape for starting and building a small business is rich. Many people are concerned that because of the current financial crisis, now may not be a good time to start a business. While it may seem counterintuitive, a recessionary climate can actually be an ideal time to start a business. In fact, many of today's popular name brands started as small companies in a down economy, such as Hyatt Corporation, Burger King, FedEx, MTV, and CNN. HP (Hewlett-Packard) was founded in a garage in Palo Alto at the end of the Great Depression. Microsoft was started in a sluggish economy by college dropout Bill Gates, and the company did just over $16,000 in revenue in its first year. Compare that to the $60 billion or so the company earns today.

So you may be wondering what it is about a down economy that serves as a fertile environment for start-ups. The founders saw a market need and created a way to fill that need. (There is much more about this in forthcoming chapters.) You could be the next big brand success.

And the best part about starting your own business is: It doesn't matter how old you are. Two of the fastest growing groups of business owners are the Gen Yers and the Baby Boomers. Both groups are often being shut out of traditional employment, so they are creating and designing their own destinies.

What does all this mean? It signifies that America is becoming a society of the self-employed. Yet most, regardless of their level of achievement in the business world, are unequipped to start and build a successful business. That's why more than half of all small businesses fail in the first three years. Moving from the security of being a W-2 employee to the topsy-turvy world of being your own boss is a significant life change and a huge challenge.

Corporate employees work hard to meet the goals and objectives of their organizations, just as small-business owners do. But that's where the similarity ends. Unlike small-business owners, corporate employees never have to worry about making a payroll or keeping the lights on. Most often, corporate employees have nice benefit packages, which include health and retirement plans. As an employee, there's no stress about accounts receivable because the corporate accounting department handles those. Bad press, a missed deadline, or a failed project can certainly create turmoil and stress in the corporate world, but when those happen to a small-business owner or entrepreneur, it can mean the end of the road. Entrepreneurs and small-business owners don't have a safety net. If there's a screwup, there's no one to bear the responsibility but themselves.

I'm not trying to discourage you from launching your own business endeavor—in fact, quite the opposite. I want to be your advocate and mentor should you decide to start up on your own. However, I also want to make sure you make your decision with your eyes wide open. If you choose to believe the motivational gurus who tell you "just follow your heart and you'll succeed," I wish you luck. If that's the case, put this book down now, because it's not for you. It is important to love what you do, whether you are an employee or an owner, but loving the work isn't enough to build a successful business.

As I've mentioned, what you *don't* know about running a business can and will hurt you. You need information to make smart business decisions for yourself and your business. This need for information starts the moment you conceptualize your business venture, and it extends all the way to when you exit the business, far down the road.

Success in your own small-business venture greatly depends on your willingness to learn, to work hard, and to focus on getting it right. That's what this book is all about—getting it *right!*

I Wish I Had Known . . .

I asked some of my Facebook friends to share what they wish they'd known before they started their businesses.

Karen Krymski: "Wish I would have had great entrepreneur mentors . . . especially financial ones, who could have helped me build a stronger biz model."

Bonny Filandrinos: "I was amazed at how many folks reached out to help me, and I was shocked to be plagued by terrible anxiety/panic attacks!"

Bob Rees: "Oh, come on. You have to first trip, stub your toe, fall on your face, and then get up smiling. :) It's the journey—isn't it fun? Think about it. If this was easy, everybody would be doing it. And to answer your questions, I'm still finding the answers, as there are many."

Mary Quigg: "Wish I had known how critical the right banking relationship would be. Starting out is fun and exciting. When you start growing, you need funding—and you need to get it *before* you actually need it."

Anne Maxfield: "How important it is to have great lawyers and accountants. You can't afford not to spend the money, it will just come back to bite you somewhere down the line."

Robyn O'Leary: "I believe that you need a great accoun-tant/CFO associated with the daily business. I believe that the decisions would be based more on fact than opportunity and keep you on a straighter path. Also read everything that requires a signature."

PART I

so you want to own a business
the real truth behind what it takes to succeed

Owning your own business—being your own boss—is the American dream. There is nothing like controlling your destiny by boldly committing to your own business vision. Starting and build ing a business from the ground up can be an exciting and reward ing experience.

Whether you're still dreaming about starting up or you're already open for business and struggling to reach your business destination, you don't need to make the journey alone. This book is your companion, equipping you with the insight, information, and inspiration you'll need to create the success you desire. The key is to make smart choices and informed decisions as you grow, and I'll help you do just that.

To succeed as an entrepreneur, you'll need not only a viable business idea but also the right mindset and motivation for being your own boss, along with personal resources and a passionate resolve to make the necessary effort and go the distance. In Part I of this book, we'll look at what it really takes for you to achieve success.

CHAPTER 1

---

starting a business is personal

Courage is doing what you're afraid to do. There can be no courage unless you're scared.
—Eleanor Roosevelt

A SMALL BUSINESS is more than just a way to make a living; it's a *way of living*. Joining the ranks of the self-employed is more involved than changing jobs or careers. It represents a lifestyle change, a lifestyle for which not everyone is suited. In this first chapter, I discuss the motivation for starting one's own business, the personality types for whom this is a viable path to success, and the considerations of one's personal financial situation as they relate to making this shift in lifestyle. Each factor is key, because each can have a dramatic impact on your ability to succeed in a business of your own.

What's Your Motivation?

Why do you want to start your own business?

- Are you running away from a bad situation with your current employer?

- Have you been unemployed for a while and are just looking to create income for yourself?

- Are you burned out in your current career and want to do something different with your life?

- Do you have a burning desire to start and build a successful business enterprise?

- Are you committed to doing whatever it takes to be a successful entrepreneur?

People give myriad reasons for wanting to start their own business. But not all of those reasons are good ones. Having a good reason for your efforts is crucial because your motivation for starting a business will play an important role in your ability to succeed.

For example, if your sole motivation for starting a business is to escape a job you hate, then you really need to rethink your choice. The same is true if you view self-employment as the only option for creating an income stream for yourself because you see no job opportunities on the horizon. In both situations, you aren't driven toward business ownership; rather, you're pushing yourself into it.

Remember, the grass is always greener on the other side of the fence.

Starting a business requires a huge personal and financial commitment, and it should not be something you enter into halfheartedly. There are significant differences in attitude, energy, and focus between running away from a situation and running toward an opportunity.

I've counseled many people who have lost their jobs and have come to me for advice about starting a business. It doesn't take long for me to identify the ones who are only going through the motions. They don't have the sparkle in their eyes when they talk about their business idea. It's as if they are describing someone else's situation rather than their own. I can sense that, if another job opportunity arose, they'd jump at it in a heartbeat. In fact, sometimes they'll even ask me to let them know if I hear of any job opportunities that might be a good fit for them. Someone who is genuinely interested in building a small business would never say that. No way.

People who start a business as their "Plan B" are quick to throw in the towel, to close up shop. If you're not entirely enthusiastic and totally committed to your business idea, you won't have the stamina to stick with and nurture your venture so it grows. Customers and clients will sense the lackluster commitment, and that doesn't foster confidence and trust. No one wants to do business with someone they believe is going to bail once a better deal comes along. Cus - tomers and clients want to know you are committed and that you will always have their best interests in mind.

Successful entrepreneurs are driven; they're passionate about their business ideas. They derive energy from the excitement of building something from scratch. They see opportunities all around them, and they have a strong desire to control their own destiny. Although initially they may not have all the information they need to get started, that doesn't deter them. They have an inherent go-for-it attitude. Determination and commitment create an insatiable desire to learn, to build, and to grow a business. Far from being a halfhearted attempt, the effort becomes their life's work. They don't just give it a try and "hope" it will work out. They are confident that they have what it takes to turn their dream into reality.

So, before you decide to strike out on your own, think about your motivation. Do you truly want to be self-employed? Are you sincerely motivated to build a business from the ground up? If you hesitate when you answer these questions, then you'll be wise to give yourself more time for careful consideration.

Do You Have the Right Stuff?

There is something alluring about the idea of being your own boss. You don't have to deal with office politics. There's no more punching a clock. You can manage your day however you choose. You can take a long lunch hour or go on an afternoon outing with your friends. There's no one to check up on you, so why not? There's no need to be concerned about the number of sick days or vacation days you have because when you are on your own—no one is counting. Yes, it sounds like the ideal work situation. However, too much freedom can be a disadvantage if you don't have the right personality to manage your time well.

While every business owner is unique, certain characteristics appear frequently among successful entrepreneurs. These traits include things such as drive, strategic thinking ability, excellent communication skills, technical knowledge, a positive attitude, independent thinking, and creativity.

Entrepreneurs and small-business owners are often described as contrarians. That is, they march to a different drummer, and are often described as eccentric. They are independent thinkers and risk takers; they're resilient and innovative.

I've been both an entrepreneur and a high-level corporate executive at a Fortune 100 company. However, I never felt comfortable in the traditional career world. I hate bureaucracy, and I roll my eyes at the thought of playing the corporate game. I never understood the rationale for a lot of the big-company policies that seemed to be inefficient and burdensome—and that doesn't begin to touch on my feelings about corporate hierarchy and protocol.

One company I worked for assigned office space based on a person's level of management. First-level managers occupied a cubicle with a certain amount of square footage and were allowed one guest chair. As you moved up the management ladder, your space was enlarged, and tables and many chairs were added. If you were fortunate enough to make it to the executive level, your ultimate reward was an actual office with a window and a door. While all this nonsense had significant meaning in the corporate world, it meant nothing in the real world. I never ran into anyone who seemed impressed that I had a corner office with its own conference table and ornate furnishings. Those things are just physical trappings—meaningless in the outside world. (By the way, those spiffy furnishings were in sharp contrast to many offices I've had as a business owner.)

In a small company, even if you're the CEO you're part of the team. No job is beneath you. You do what you need to do to accomplish your goals. Whereas in the typical corporate environment, you follow the chain of command even if that isn't the most expedient or prudent way to manage the task at hand. That's why large corporations can't respond as quickly to opportunities as small businesses can.

When you become self-employed, you have to be willing to relinquish the trappings of corporate life. Instead of being given a job title with defined responsibilities, you will be the chief cook and bottle washer. Everything falls on your plate, and you execute without a predetermined budget, support staff, or fancy office. In fact, new businesses are frequently launched in a garage or spare bedroom, with cardboard boxes functioning as file cabinets and a folding table serving as a desk. One of my businesses back in the late '80s was called Wilson & Associates, the "associates" being my two cats, with my guest room serving as corporate headquarters.

The truth is, starting a business is a test of strategy, stamina, commitment, and resilience. It's like being on the TV show *Survivor*—a game of survival of the fittest. But there is nothing glamorous about starting a business; it's just hard work. And without the right personality for participation, you won't win that game. So, it's not enough just to have the right motivation for starting a business. Before you go any further, you need to determine whether or not you have the right "stuff."

It takes a certain personality type to function comfortably and well as an entrepreneur. Business basics can be learned, but not everyone has the personality to flourish on his or her own. There's no shame in being ill-suited for being in business for yourself, but be honest with yourself now, before you make the leap and find it's too late to turn back.

Do you have the right stuff to be an entrepreneur? To help you decide, I've compiled a personality assessment. As you're responding to each statement, be brutally honest with yourself. No one is judging you and you aren't being graded. The assessment, which appears on the facing page, is for your benefit only. Answer each statement with a "yes" or "no."

How many questions did you answer with a yes? The more yes answers, the greater your chances are of succeeding in your own business.

If only ten of your answers were yes, then building your own business will present challenges for you, but it won't be impossible.

However, if you responded to fewer than eight statements in the affirmative, then in my opinion you should seriously consider following another path, or at least find a strong entrepreneurial partner. Here's why each of these characteristics is important:

• *Self-starter.* When you are an employee, most of your tasks are assigned by your boss. Generally, you understand what is expected of

Entrepreneurial Personality Assessment		
	YES	NO
1. I am a self-starter.		
2. I am comfortable working by myself.		
3. I am good with people.		
4. I am a risk taker.		
5. I am adept at juggling multiple tasks.		
6. I am a high-energy person.		
7. I am eager to learn new things.		
8. I am a good salesperson.		
9. I manage my time well.		
10. I have a strong personal support network.		
11. I am self-confident.		
12. I am resilient.		
13. I am comfortable making decisions.		
14. I am a strategic thinker/visionary.		
15. I am persistent.		

you, when it is to be completed, and how the work is to be performed. However, when you start your own business, there is no one telling you what to do. Not only is the work not assigned, but you have to get out and pound the pavement just to find business. That takes a lot of initiative. You'll be working in an unstructured environment where everything—from identifying the opportunities to establishing the mode of execution—rests on your shoulders. There is no blueprint to follow. In many respects, you're making it up as you go.

• *Enjoy working by yourself.* Most start-ups are one-person shows. In fact, many companies today start off as home-based businesses. When you don't have a co-worker with whom to kibitz in the next cubicle or in the coffee room, you may feel isolated. Some people who get energized by engaging and brainstorming with others often report feeling depressed or de-motivated when they try to go it alone. Such feelings diminish productivity and limit your ability to succeed. People who fare best during the initial start-up stages of a business are those who don't mind working on their own.

• *People person.* If you aren't a "people person," then being in business for yourself will be difficult, if not impossible. (Being a "people person" is not the same as preferring to have people around with whom to chat. You can work well alone and still be a "people person.") When you are self-employed, *you* are the business. Regardless of how great your product or service is, people do business with people they like and trust. Therefore, your ability to build relationships with customers is integral to your business success. If you are more of a behind-the-scenes person, consider hiring someone or bringing in a partner who can be the "face" of the business and can interact easily and comfortably with your customers and clients.

• *Risk taker.* Building a business from the ground up is risky. It involves risks both personal and financial. Again, the majority of small businesses fail within the first three years. Those are daunting odds, so you need to be able to go beyond your comfort zone, rolling the dice and going for it. If you're starting a business and the thought of taking risks keeps you up at night—then be prepared for many sleepless nights.

• *Multitasker.* When you start a business, you're responsible for doing nearly everything yourself. Not everyone functions well with so many balls in the air. It can be very stressful. In the initial stages of business growth, there never seem to be enough hours to get everything done. You produce the product or provide the service, and at the same time you're handling the bookkeeping and functioning as the sales force. That's a lot of juggling. I'm going to go out on a limb here and say that most entrepreneurs are stress junkies: They thrive on working under pressure. You know the saying about how if you want something done, give it to the busiest person? That's me. For some reason, I perform better when I have many things going at the same time.

• *High-energy.* Starting a business requires an infinite amount of energy. You only *think* you've worked hard in previous jobs. Wait until you go out on your own. To be successful, you will have to exert 150 percent of your time and effort. The business is with you all the time. But there is something about knowing that everything rests on your shoulders that can push you into perennial overdrive. Some people say they want to start their own businesses because they want more balance in their lives and more control over their schedules. They are being naïve. To be successful in your own business, you have to work harder and longer than you have ever worked in your life. That's why being a high-energy person is essential.

• *Eager to learn.* When you start a business, you most likely choose something you enjoy and something at which you are good. However, no matter how good you are at doing what you do, you probably don't know a lot about the fundamentals of starting and growing a business from the ground up. Therefore, you must be willing to listen and learn, and to acquire some solid business principles and practices. Too often, entrepreneurs think they can do it all themselves. Unfortunately, that attitude gets them in trouble. Smart start-ups understand the importance of getting the right advice and learning what it takes to build a business—and not just how to deliver to the market a specific product or service. I firmly believe that an eagerness to learn is one of the most important building blocks of business success. I'll talk more about why this is critical in subsequent chapters.

• *Good salesperson.* Don't consider yourself a salesperson? When you start your own business, you'd better. No one can sell your business better than you can. To be successful, you'll find yourself selling all the time. So if the thought of making a sales call sends shivers down your spine, you're going to have a tough time growing your business.

• *Time manager.* Because building a business heaps so many demands on your time, your time-management skill is crucial. New businesses tend to have unstructured environments. Failing to use your time efficiently will reduce your ability to achieve your business goals.

I see many new owners procrastinating. They bury themselves in busy work, like checking emails or running errands, instead of focusing on the important activities that will drive their business. Time gets away from them, and then those critical actions are put off for a day, a week, or even months. If you're not efficient with your time, your business will suffer. As they say, time is money.

• *Strong personal support network.* It's tough to start a new business venture without the support of your friends and family. The pressures of building a business are stressful enough without having to deal with people close to you complaining about how much time you're devoting to it, or knocking you down for trying to build something. You need people around you who will be there to cheer you on and who will understand the personal sacrifices being successful will require.

• *Self-confident.* You are going to hear the word "no" a lot, so it's helpful to have thick skin. Though business experts advise you not to take things personally, it's hard not to when dealing with your own business. That's because when you're putting so much of yourself on the line for it, it's difficult to separate the business from who you are personally. If you run short on self-confidence, you're going to be uncomfortable in your own business. Customers and clients need confidence in your ability to deliver a quality product or service. Your future employees will expect you to be a confident leader. If you lack confidence in yourself, how can you expect others to have confidence in your business?

• *Resilient.* I was invited to lunch with a group of college-level business and entrepreneurial students to talk about what it's like to be in business for yourself. One of the young men asked me what I believed to be the most important criterion for success. I said "Resilience." No matter how well you plan your business launch, you're going to encounter obstacles and setbacks. (In fact, lots of successful business owners experienced at least one business failure before they became successful.) But instead of dwelling on failure, successful entrepreneurs pick themselves up and move on. As someone once said, the mark of a true success is someone who hits rock bottom but bounces back even higher than before.

• *Decision maker.* Business owners absolutely must be comfortable making decisions on their own; otherwise, nothing will get done. If you're one of those people who hems and haws and can never seem to make up your mind, then running a business is not for you. In business you must be decisive. Taking too long to make up your mind can mean lost opportunities and seriously negative consequences for your business.

• *Strategic thinker/visionary.* Strategic thinkers make good entrepreneurs because they don't dwell on detail. They're people who can see the big picture and determine what needs to be done to get from point A to point Z. They see an opportunity and move forward to seize the moment. Successful entrepreneurs think big even though they start small. (I'll discuss this more later.) In other words, if you can't envision what you want your business to become, it will be difficult for you to map out the steps needed to create a successful, sustainable enterprise.

• *Persistent.* If at first you don't succeed, try, try again. Successful business owners understand that it takes persistent effort to make their businesses work. It takes discipline to work on moving the business forward every day, and a commitment to doing whatever needs to be done to reach their goals. Take, for example, the business owner who was told by her delivery company that a big order would not arrive as scheduled because a snowstorm had stalled the truck. Determined not to let a mere blizzard cause her company to fail, she located the truck, got behind the wheel, backed it out the wrong way down a one-way street, and managed to arrive on time at her client's doorstep. Now, that's persistence.

Legend has it that it took Thomas Edison 1,000 attempts to invent the lightbulb. And it's been said he claimed that he did not fail 999 times, but rather he learned 999 ways in which not to make a lightbulb. Renowned inventor and businessman Charles F. Kettering commented, "An inventor fails 999 times, and if he succeeds once, he's in. He treats his failures simply as practice shots." Bottom line: If you're going to succeed, you can't be one who gives up quickly.

The Financial Realities of Starting a Business

Jumping into self-employment without first understanding the effect it will have on your personal financial situation is a serious mistake. Too many business start-ups I've dealt with haven't taken the time to calculate the real financial impact on themselves, personally. I think a lot of people mistakenly believe that when they start the business, there will be money coming in right away. Yes, let's hope there will be some revenue soon, but probably not enough to remain in your pocket.

From a personal financial perspective, there are three major questions you need to consider: (1) How much money are you comfortable losing? (2) How long can you go without an income from your business? and (3) How will you recover if the business fails?

How Much Money Can You Afford to Lose?

Some people are willing to gamble everything they've got to get their business off the ground. They are so committed to their idea and their vision that nothing else matters. Reckless? Perhaps. There are many stories of people who were on the brink of bankruptcy and refused to give up their dream—but their persistence, determination, and passion paid off because they hung in there and were able to go the distance. Of course, there are even more stories in which the opposite is true.

Other potential small-business owners don't want to risk any of their own assets. Often, people tell me that they don't have any money to start their business, or they simply don't want to invest any of their own funds, so they want to know how to find investors or how to get a loan. Note: No one is going to invest in your business if you don't have a significant amount of skin in the game. You've got to put your money on the line, too.

There's no mathematical formula that suggests how much money you should invest in your new business. That answer depends on your own circumstances. However, you should know that start-ups rarely get funded by using other people's money. That's particularly true if you are a first-time business owner, without a track record of success.

How Long Can You Survive Without a Paycheck?

In their early stages, most businesses don't generate enough money to pay the business owner a salary, so in your financial assessment you need to consider the likely loss of income.

"I had to sell my car to get some money to do this business. I sold everything I could think of. I looked around my house to see what, if anything, was worth anything in here. I even had to sell a ring that was very dear to me. It was given to me by my grandfather 30 years ago," shares Paula Bennett-Aromando, a recently divorced mother who launched Bling Jeans Company. "It's not just a matter of making a business run; you have to make a life run at the same time, and that is very trying at times."

Most financial experts recommend that you have at least six to twelve months of living expenses saved before you launch your business. (Some people say three months, but I don't think that's realistic.) If you have a spouse or domestic partner who can support you or share expenses for a while, that will certainly make the transition from a W-2 employee to business owner easier. But it also means that whoever is going to cover the bills for a while needs to be as committed to your business success as you are. Set realistic expectations in terms of how long it may take before you can generate an income again, keeping in mind that it always takes longer than you think it will. Do a personal financial review and create a budget. Without your income, you may need to do some belt-tightening.

What Is Your "Plan B" if Your Business Fails?

Yes, it's important to think positively about your business venture. But I do encourage you to be a realist, and as such you should have a worst-case scenario. So what are you going to do if your business fails? You've lost the financial investment. You've lost time building a traditional career. Can you live with the consequences?

Consider your age. How long do you have to rebound financially from a failed business? The younger you are, the better your chances are of recovering. Be very careful about using retirement savings for the initial capital your business needs, especially if you are over 40. Beyond a certain point, it becomes difficult to rebuild your retirement nest egg. Also, keep in mind the taxes and penalties that may be imposed should you decide to tap into those funds. I know that when you need money to get started it is tempting to dip into that pot, particularly when you are confident your business is going to be a success. But remember, the odds are not in your favor. There are plenty of people working at jobs they hate today because they used their retirement savings to fund a business that didn't work out—and now they need a paycheck in order to survive.

Your Personal Credit Rating

Although it is difficult to obtain financing for a start-up business, it is not impossible. However, if you are seeking funding to start your business, make sure your personal credit is in good standing. Your personal credit rating will also be important for establishing credit with a landlord or vendors.

If you don't know what your credit rating is, you can obtain one free credit report annually from each of the major credit rating agencies: Equifax, Experian, and TransUnion. I recommend spreading the reports out over the course of the year to keep track of activity on your account.

Once you receive your credit report, review it to make sure it's accurate. If you find errors on the report, get them corrected. If you have a low score, now is the time to try to improve it. If there are particular issues that have damaged your credit history, such as medical bills due to a catastrophic illness, you may be able to explain the situation to a potential lender, investor, vendor, or landlord. However, it is best to clean up your credit report before you get too far along with your business endeavor.

Here are the credit-report agency websites:

www.equifax.com

www.experian.com

www.transunion.com

A Final Note

Entrepreneurship has its advantages and disadvantages, its risks and rewards. One of the advantages is you never have to wait for permission to try new ideas. You can act quickly. If the idea doesn't work, you can drop it just as easily. This kind of flexibility can be great and provides a significant competitive advantage for a small business. But it also has a major downside. What if your idea is such a flop that it costs you a significant amount of money? And perhaps even worse, your professional reputation. You may not have the ability to overcome the mistake, and as a result, you could be forced to go out of business.

As your business grows, you'll probably find the need to add employees, and that means you'll have to meet a payroll, week after week. In addition, your company will need sufficient cash flow to pay creditors as well as fund your working capital needs. All of these things must take priority over writing yourself a paycheck.

Moreover, you'll face adverse situations—many caused by circumstances beyond your control. Overcoming these setbacks and keeping your business profitable will require long hours of hard work—and maybe not the kind of work you want to do. But, again, you can forget about work/life balance in the early years.

Keep in mind that starting a business is a lifestyle change, just like making a decision to lose weight and get healthy. To be successful, you need to make a long-term commitment to the process and stick with it. We know yo-yo diets don't work. Neither do businesses that lack the personal commitment of the founder. You need not only the right mindset, motivation, and personal resources, but also the resolve to go the distance.

Notwithstanding all that I have said up to this point, one thing I can tell you for sure is that starting and growing a business of your own is the most rewarding experience you'll ever have. It's your baby. Other than maybe being president of the United States, I can't imagine a position in which you can feel as empowered. And when it works—when you get it right—WOW!

CHAPTER 2

---

make smart choices
consider your options

NOW THAT YOU have an overview of what it takes to start and grow a successful small business, you may be having second thoughts. *Good.* You are thinking carefully about making this major decision. Now is a good time to introduce a few options that can help you minimize your risk if you choose to get into business for yourself.

Don't Go Cold Turkey: Begin Part-Time

Consider testing the waters by starting your business on a part-time basis. If you currently have a full-time position, you may be able to begin by working on your business during your own time; for most people, that's evenings and weekends. But there are a few key things to be mindful of if you decide to moonlight with your own business.

First, don't do the kind of work that would conflict or compete with your current employer unless you have fully disclosed it and obtained your boss's permission; otherwise, it could be grounds for immediate termination. On the other hand, there are examples of employers who have helped employees build their own businesses. This may be your case if there are projects too small for your current employer and they are something your new business could handle on the side. Your employer might refer those opportunities to you, giving you an opportunity to build experience and a clientele.

Second, don't let your part-time business interfere with the work you are doing for your current employer. Remember, whenever you are "at work" you are obligated to focus on only those tasks that benefit your employer. Stealing a little time from your employer to work on your own part-time business is just that—stealing. That, too, can be grounds for termination.

Keep in mind that while this venture may be a part-time business for you, your customers or clients are going to expect your full attention and professional results. So don't set expectations that you can't deliver, or take on more than you can handle. That's an easy way to get a bad reputation for your business, which can be difficult to overcome and a serious problem if you decide to make your business a full-time venture.

Manage your part-time business just like a "real" business—because it is. Set up a bookkeeping system so you can keep your business income and expenses separate from your personal records. Make sure you have the appropriate permits and licenses. Create professional-looking marketing materials and a website.

You may find, as many people do, that your part-time business will grow and flourish and bring you to a decision point: whether to stay with your current employer, keeping your business small enough to manage, or take the big step and quit your job to focus on the growth of your business. At this point, at least you'll know whether or not you enjoy the challenge of running a business on your own, which should guide you in making the right choice.

A Part-Time Success Story

Twin brothers Randy and Jeff Vines grew up in the suburbs of St. Louis, but at a very young age they fell in love with the history, culture, diversity, and even the quirkiness of the city of St. Louis. On Saturdays, while most teenage suburbanites were hanging around the shopping malls, the Vines brothers would hop on a city bus and spend the day producing a local-access television show on city life.

"The people in the city are just a notch above. They have swagger you just don't see everywhere," explains Randy Vines.

While away at college, the brothers wanted to display their civic pride and show off the unique character of their beloved city via their clothing. But the only apparel available was typical tourist attire—not exactly what they had in mind. Then, back in St. Louis with traditional jobs, the Vines brothers still longed for edgy, trendy apparel depicting the colorfulness of St. Louis, so they decided to create their own. Almost immediately, they knew they were onto something big.

"When we would wear our own designs, we'd be asked by strangers on the street, 'Where did you get that shirt?'" remembers Jeff Vines. "So we did a small run and then signed up to have a booth at some downtown festivals, and we always would sell out quickly. We learned real quick what people wanted."

That was the beginning of STL-Style. Mostly selling out of boxes in the back of their car, the Vines's T-shirt creations became a big hit, garnering extensive press coverage, including an article in the *New York Times*. Soon people were ordering from around the world, and it was difficult to keep up with demand. While continuing to work their "day jobs," the two committed their nights and weekends to their burgeoning business.

"There weren't enough hours in the day. We had to hire our friends to help out part-time, and it became a matter of whether we were going to keep treading water and doing what we were doing or were we going to take this to the next level and get serious about it," Jeff says.

After nine years of part-time operations, testing the market, and developing new products, the Vines twins decided to turn their part-time passion into a full-time enterprise. As Randy notes, "I think more and more, the culture in America is about taking less conventional approaches to earning a living. More than ever, there is this excitement about entrepreneurism and people are figuring out a way to turn their passion into dollar signs."

A part-time business gives you the opportunity to develop your business model and learn from your mistakes. Randy and Jeff Vines waited until the business basically directed their decision for them. It had gone as far as it could go as a part-time endeavor. That's a pivotal point many part-time businesses reach, and if you decide then to pursue the business full-time, you aren't starting from ground zero. You already have history and experience from which to grow, and that minimizes your risk.

A Franchise May Be a Start-Up Shortcut

Starting a business from scratch is difficult. You have to figure out everything on your own, and in the process you inevitably make mistakes—some of them costly, some of them just frustrating. Let's hope none result in the loss of your business, but there is always a level of inherent risk involved.

Buying a franchise minimizes the risk of getting started in business. A franchise operation is, in many respects, a business in a box. It comes with a set of instructions, so to speak, including customized training and ongoing support. Whether it's with accounting and financing, advertising and public relations, personnel management, purchasing, or inventory control, the franchise organization is there to assist you and help you succeed. As a franchisee, you are in business for yourself, but not *by* yourself. In return for this assistance, you typically pay an initial fee and ongoing royalties to the franchise organization.

While there are many excellent franchise opportunities available today, don't be lulled into a false sense of security. Just as with any other business opportunity, you need to do your homework; you need to make sure the franchise is a good personal choice, as well as a smart financial decision.

If you like doing things your own way, however, then a franchise won't be a good fit for you. To protect its brand and maintain consistency, the franchise organization expects its franchisees to do business their way. So if you don't follow their system, depending on the terms of your contract, you run the risk of losing your franchise. For some people, the thought of giving up even a little control is out of the question. So if you have a strong entrepreneurial spirit, then becoming a franchisee probably isn't your best bet.

However, if you do choose this approach, make sure you invest in a solid franchise operation. If you are seriously considering the purchase of a franchise, review the document called the Uniform Franchise Offering Circular (UFOC). The Federal Trade Com-mission (FTC) requires any franchise organization to provide you with this document; this is known as the "Franchise Rule." In the document, you'll find detailed information about the franchising company, including financial statements, past or pending litigation, bankruptcies, and a list of existing franchises. Ask the franchise organization lots of questions. Secure professional help to review the document as well. And by all means, talk to existing franchisees.

In addition to doing the normal due diligence, make sure the franchise you are considering is a good fit for your particular area. Not every franchise opportunity works in every geographic area. For example, have you ever visited a different part of the country and stumbled on a particular franchised restaurant that you enjoyed, and thought how you'd love to have one where you live? Maybe you think the restaurant would flourish in your area—but there may be a very good reason there aren't any in your community. Considerations such as population density, ethnic characteristics, the socioeconomic makeup of an area, and even the climate may all be important factors in determining whether or not a franchise will be successful in a particular region.

In addition to location, long-term appeal of the franchise product or service is important. Is the business based on a fad? Fads are fleeting, and you don't want your investment to fizzle out because the product or service has lost its popularity.

Find out, also, what is expected of you other than your financial commitment. For example, what type of experience is required? Some franchises don't expect you to have any experience in the industry, but they may require that you spend considerable time in training to learn their system. For example, McDonald's and its famous Hamburger University.

You'll also need to know what kind of work hours and personal commitment will be expected of you in order to run the franchise successfully. One franchise organization I consulted with a number of years ago required that their franchisees be owner/operators. In other words, the buyer of the franchise needed to be at the location most of the time. That may not be a good fit for your lifestyle.

Finally, if you choose to invest in a franchise system, know your rights. Consult with an attorney before you close the deal to make sure you are protected.

Buy an Existing Business

Many would-be business owners prefer the idea of purchasing an already existing business. Certainly, buying a business is significantly less risky than starting one from scratch. But just as if you were starting with an original business concept, the first question you must ask yourself is: Is this a business I'd feel good about and enjoy? Do I have adequate experience in this type of business or industry to be successful? If the answer is "no," then, it doesn't matter if the business is a sure thing—it's not the right fit for you.

There are several ways to identify a potential business opportunity for sale. One way is through a business broker, who works much like a real estate agent, except he or she specializes in listing and selling businesses instead of properties. However, not all business brokers are created equal. Research the brokerage company before you pursue any listing. Make sure the company and the representative are legitimate. Also, keep in mind that, just as in real estate, the broker is representing the seller, not your interests. If you get serious about pursuing a business opportunity, you need to obtain independent counsel to protect your interests.

You can also learn about businesses for sale from other business owners or from professional advisers. A lot of businesses don't want to broadcast the fact that they are for sale, for fear of losing their customers and their employees; therefore, the potential sale is handled more discreetly. For example, the business owner may confide in his CPA that he is interested in selling. The CPA, who works with a lot of other clients, may be aware of someone who is searching for a business in which to invest. The CPA may also confidentially mention it to other professionals with whom she works.

Another option is to do a little legwork on your own if you know the type of business you are interested in. Have you ever driven through a neighborhood when you were in the market for a house and found one you fell in love with, even though it wasn't for sale? Maybe you watched and waited for a while to see if it would become available, or perhaps you were bold enough to knock on the door and share your interest with the owner. You never know unless you ask. So apply the same technique to your business search. Drive through the business neighborhood, so to speak, and identify businesses of interest. Then ask around, because you just never know. In fact, sometimes you may find a business owned by someone who is reaching retirement age and who has no succession plan in place. In that case, you may be able to purchase the business and work out an agreement whereby the retiring owner remains active for a period of time. That gives you the advantage of learning from the previous owner and allowing for a smooth transition with employees and customers.

Buying a business can certainly ease your entry into the world of entrepreneurship, but you still have to be smart about it. Even if a business seems to be financially sound, if you don't know anything about the business you could have problems, because usually there won't be anyone around to train you. Take note of the nature of the business. If it is a business built on personal relationships, it may be difficult to sustain those relationships once the original owner is gone.

Before you make a buying decision, do your homework. Dig into the financials and ask questions. You especially want to know why the owner is selling. That may be the most important question you ask. Perhaps there is something going on that isn't apparent in the business records. For example, I once heard about a business for sale that, by all indications, looked like an excellent deal. But when the prospective buyer did additional research, talking to some other business owners in the area, he learned that a bridge that served as the primary way in and out of the region was going to be closed for repairs for about a year. Imagine what a serious impact that would have on the business.

Remember that buying an existing business can be expensive. Generally, the rule of thumb is that for every $100,000 of personal income you want to take out of the business, you'll pay five times that amount for the business. In today's economy, banks are seldom willing to make loans for the purchase of an existing business, so you might need to seek seller financing. You should consider it a positive sign if a seller is willing to finance the sale with a minimum down payment. It demonstrates that the owner has faith in the sustainability of the business.

• • •

These are a few of the ways in which you can join the small-business community without building a business from the ground up. However, as I noted in the previous chapter, your mindset, motivation, determination, and personality are integral factors in your ability to succeed. In addition, the business-building principles in the subsequent chapters will be equally important to the health of your new venture.

venture will suit you best. In the previous chapter I discussed various ways to dip your toe in the water by sampling other business forms; here, I talk about jumping in the deep end of the pool—originating and developing your new business from scratch.

At this stage of the process, people wanting to start a business usually fall into one of three categories: (1) those who already have a business idea and are eager to get going; (2) those who have multiple ideas, but haven't yet settled on "the one"; and (3) those who want to own a business but have no idea what to do.

Frankly, this last category makes me nervous because immediately I would question the person's commitment. You'd be amazed at how many people have asked *me* to tell *them* what kind of business they should start. No one, including me, is equipped to tell someone else what type of business to get going. I can tell you what industries are hot, or what trends I see, but your choice of business has to be something that is a good fit for you.

For example, my husband once thought about buying an HVAC company, even though he isn't the handiest guy around the house, and he knew very little about HVAC systems. Nor does he have a burning desire to learn more about them. Could he have been successful operating the HVAC business? Maybe. After all, he's a smart guy. But he'd never be as successful in the HVAC business as if he had found a business opportunity that used his strengths and was something that he enjoyed learning about and doing. His lack of knowledge—and perhaps more important, his lack of *interest*—would most likely lead to a disappointing outcome.

So don't be swayed by how promising a business opportunity may seem to others; the critical factor is whether or not the business is right for you. Taking into account your knowledge base, your interests, and what you enjoy doing will help you beat the odds when you start your business. It has been said that if you love what you do, you'll never work a day in your life. That's a situation worth planning for.

CHAPTER 3

---

beat the odds
get it right from the beginning

ONE REASON MANY small-business ventures fail is that the founder isn't sufficiently compatible with the choice of business. In other words, she finds out—too late—that she doesn't "love it" as she thought she would. It's hard to devote 150 percent of your effort to the business if you aren't passionate about what you are doing.

Once you've decided that becoming your own boss is the right option for you, your next step is to determine what type of business

Start with Something You Know—or Go for a Test Drive

Sounds obvious, but the best place to begin your entrepreneurial journey is with something you know. If you have a skill or a product that is marketable, then that's your logical entry point. There is going to be so much you'll have to learn about running a business that the more you know about the product or service itself, the easier it will be for you.

Many business failures can easily be attributed to a lack of managerial experience and knowledge. However, a lot of people go into business because they want to do something new and exciting. So if your business idea is in an area in which you have little or no experience, try it out first. Volunteer with an organization or company to get some related experience. If there are opportunities available, consider a part-time, or even a full-time, job in the field. A business may look interesting, but once you get involved with it on a day-to-day basis, you may come to find that you hate it! It's better to discover that before you invest your time, talent, and resources.

For example, for many people who enjoy cooking and entertaining, owning a restaurant looks like it would be fun. From all outward appearances, the restaurant business seems glamorous—especially when you see the owner of an established venue mixing with the customers, shaking hands, and working the room. Add to that the rise of celebrity chefs, and it makes the business look even more exciting. But the restaurant business is difficult. It requires long hours, including nights, weekends, and holidays. It's a business in which employee turnover is high and theft is common. Competition is fierce, and the market is fickle. You can be the hot spot one week and find yourself with empty tables the next. Without experience in the restaurant or hospitality industry, you wouldn't have insight into the behind-the-scenes difficulties that restaurateurs regularly encounter.

By working in and familiarizing yourself with the business or industry you are considering, you can avoid making novice mistakes.

For example, a lot of new restaurant owners close their doors quickly because they simply hadn't planned for the difficulty in hiring and retaining qualified staff. But someone who has restaurant experience, or who has worked in a related business, will be familiar with the high employee turnover and know how to judge good job candidates. In short, there are nuances to every type of business, and as an owner, the more familiar you are with the potential problems, the better equipped you will be to deal with them.

Never rush to judgment when you launch your business. Gather as much information as you can in advance, and don't be embarrassed or hesitant to ask for assistance from trusted advisers, mentors, or professionals when you need it. I wish I had a dime for every business owner who has ever said "If only I'd known. . . ."

The bottom line: When you start a new endeavor, there's a lot you won't know, so it's important to bring as much to the party as you can—at least when it comes to the type of business you choose.

Finally, if you lack related business experience, and there's no opportunity for you to obtain some, consider partnering with someone who *is* experienced. While a fresh outlook on a business can be a good thing, because it fosters innovative ideas, a seasoned partner can help you avoid the less obvious pitfalls. With your complementary strengths, together you may create the Next Big Thing.

Passion Doesn't Equal Profit

"If you're passionate about what you do, you can't help but succeed." *Oh yes, you can!* Yet, there are so many business books and popular speakers who want to feed you this line of B.S. *Forget whatever else you've read.* If you get nothing else from this book, pay close attention to this sentence: Passion is not the singular key to business success. Let me repeat: *Passion is not the singular key to business success!*

Sure, the passion thing sounds good (and easy), and I'm sure it sells a lot of motivational books, CDs, and seminars. But it's not the whole enchilada. Believing that passion by itself is the key to business success is like thinking sappy chick flicks reflect real life. Anyone who has built a successful business understands that it requires a lot more than passion.

Don't get me wrong. Passion is one of the important ingredients for success—in everything you do. It is life's energy source. Without a high level of enjoyment in the work you do, you won't have the energy and the drive you need to get you over the inevitable hurdles you will face in your new business. Furthermore, when you love something and are passionate about it, it's easier to excel.

Think about successful athletes. They practice hours and hours each day, despite aches and pains or inclement weather. Their lives are focused on improving their game so that they can be serious competitors. They have a special talent and passion for the sport, which provides them with the necessary energy, but it is their commitment and dedication to it that set them apart from the rest of us.

The same is true in business. Success depends on practicing the business fundamentals daily: keeping your eye on the goal, being willing to be coached, and maintaining a strong, committed work ethic. There are lots of passionate people in the world who never achieve their goals. That's because building a business is plain old hard work! And if you don't have the discipline to get up and go after it every single day, then you're not going to be successful. After all, if it were that easy, every new business would be a success.

The Best Business Idea Starts with a Problem

Show me a problem, and I'll show you a business opportunity. Starting a business that's the same-old, same-old stuff makes it tough to capture people's attention. "Me too" business ideas rarely become great businesses. The businesses most likely to take off are created by entrepreneurs who see a need in the market that isn't currently being met, and who figure out a way to meet that need. Now, that might mean inventing a new product, creating a new industry, or simply figuring out a better way to provide a service or bring a product to market.

Belts to the Rescue

Former social worker turned inventor Talia Goldfarb needed a belt to hold her potty-training son's pants up when he wasn't wearing a diaper—one that he could easily manage on his own. After her sister and she searched everywhere to no avail, they decided to create one on their own. The result: Myself Belts. A cleverly designed belt that snaps around one of the kid's belt loops and uses Velcro as a fastener. Goldfarb told me she couldn't believe no one else had thought of the idea because it was so simple. Myself Belts are now in more than 700 stores around the world, and they are available on the Internet, where the founders say they do the majority of their business.

A Trans-Mission

A successful entrepreneur sees a market opportunity and creates an entirely new type of business. Anthony Martino recognized that eventually most cars would need transmission repair or replacement. And while car dealerships and gas stations focused on selling cars and gasoline, respectively, he realized that no one was focusing on transmissions—so he launched AAMCO Transmission Services. His franchise became the world's largest transmission specialists.

Shoes on Demand

You are probably familiar with the popular Internet shoe site Zappos. Founder Nick Swinmurn certainly didn't invent shoes— or the Internet. He simply changed the way people purchase shoes. Frustrated with department-store offerings and unable to find his favorite boot in the right size and color, Swinmurn developed an idea. Instead of hoofing it all over the place, why not create an online megastore that would offer shoes in all styles, colors, and sizes? For busy and frustrated customers like himself, he provided something a traditional retail store could not offer—a virtually stress-free environment in which to shop for shoes.

From Dimes to Dollars

Sam Walton approached the Ben Franklin dime-store chain in the early '60s about his idea of establishing discount business operations. He recognized a unique market need, but Ben Franklin's management didn't. So, instead of working with the chain, Walton struck out on his own, and he opened his first Wal-Mart store on July 2, 1962, in Rogers, Arkansas. When was the last time you shopped in a Ben Franklin store? I bet there's a Wal-Mart within a couple of miles of where you live. Sam Walton didn't copy and compete; instead, he changed the nature of the business forever.

■ ■ ■

So think about your business concept in terms of solving a market problem. Where is there a gap between what customers want and what is being delivered to them? In investment circles, this is called the *market pain*. What's the pain? What's the problem that isn't being solved? And what's your solution?

Let me share a personal example. When I was a full-time broadcast journalist, I used to pitch small-business stories to my news director. Typically, my ideas fell on deaf ears. Those in mass media, particularly electronic media, didn't grasp the size of the audience for small-business features—and that it was a rapidly growing market segment. After I purchased the domain SBTV.com—small-business television—from an existing website owner, it became clear to me that I could create an electronic mass medium to serve the needs of the small-business market.

At first, we considered launching a cable network, but the funding required was beyond our reach. Furthermore, my partners and I believed that, in the near future, consumers would dictate how, when, and where they would access media resources. It wouldn't matter if you were on cable, traditional broadcast, or the Internet—the lines between the media would blur, and you could watch anything, anywhere, anytime. So we decided to create a broadcast medium on the Internet that focused on news and information for small businesses. An Internet form of CNBC for small business, of sorts. That was in January 2004, and people thought we were nuts. Television on the Internet? It will never work!

When we launched our SBTV.com website, there were other sites providing information for small businesses, but not in a video format. We defined a market need—electronic broadcast media for small business—and we identified a financially feasible way to deliver it to the market.

As you define, refine, evaluate, and develop your business idea, think about how you can deliver a product or service in a unique or different way—a way the market really wants it. How can *you* stand out from any competition?

Can You Make Money?

My mother was an outstanding businesswoman and entrepreneur. Even as her mind faded with the effects of Alzheimer's, when I discussed my business with her, she'd take my hand and ask, "But, honey, are you making any money?" Nothing like getting right to the point. You go into business to make money. That's the bottom line. Even if you invent the world's greatest mousetrap, if you can't sell it and make money, it's not a good business idea.

There's no sense in going into business if you can't anticipate making a reasonable profit. Why work as hard as you'll need to work to build a business if you're working for pennies? So as your business idea develops, your challenge becomes that of determining whether or not there is an opportunity for your venture to be profitable. At this juncture, it's premature to dive into an elaborate financial analysis of your business concept, but you should do a preliminary, back-of-the-envelope review to estimate the potential profitability and sustainability of your business idea.

First, is there a market for your product or service? You obviously think there is, but are there enough people who would be interested in buying from you? Second, will those people interested in buying your product or service also be willing to pay enough to allow you to make real money?

For example, consider a woman who enjoys cake decorating, so all her friends encourage her to start her own business. Depending on the complexity of the cake design, each cake she makes will take her from three to eight hours to complete. Suppose the woman decides she wants to charge $10 for each hour of her labor, plus the cost of her supplies; that means one of her low-end cakes would cost at least $40. Depending on the socioeconomic profile of the area in which she lives, she has to determine how many people would be willing to pay $40 for, say, a child's birthday cake, when, alternatively, they could run to the nearby big-box store and get one for considerably less.

Assuming there *is* a market for her *higher* priced cakes, how many can she produce in a day? In a week? Based on this general review, can she generate enough revenue to turn her cake decorating into a viable business? Probably not. Unless she hires other people to increase her volume and can create a process to systematize production of the cakes, her business will remain a microenterprise at best—with minimal profitability. (I'll talk more about pricing and process later.)

Third, are there other, similar types of businesses already out there? You can learn a lot from researching the competition. You may *think* you're the first one to come up with a business concept, but chances are someone else has thought of it, too. If no one else has seen the business concept take off, there may be a reason for it. Obvious issues could be market demand and price. The competitor might have learned that there isn't enough opportunity out there to build a sustainable, scalable, profitable business.

By example, consider the mobile pet-grooming services. There are lots of them popping up here and there. On the surface, this concept sounds like a reasonably good business idea. However, I called one recently to inquire about fees for grooming my two small dogs. The provider wanted $75 per animal, with a $5 discount for doing both on the same day. Call me a tightwad if you like, but in my hometown market, that's a ridiculous price. I can drive a couple of miles to a nearby groomer and get it done for less than half that price. So it causes me to question just how large the real market for this service is and how these businesses can reach a comfortable profitability level.

Whatever your idea, you have to look at the number of people who might buy your product—realistically. Let's say that in your area there are 10,000 potential customers for your product. For your business to be successful, you think you'll need to sell to 60 percent of these people. But that's going to be tough, if not impossible. On the other hand, if your business is viable with a 10 percent market share, then your chance of making a decent profit is more realistic.

Prelaunch Market Research

Conducting market research when you're just thinking about starting a business may sound costly, but there are ways in which you can do it professionally and affordably. And keep in mind that, at this prelaunch stage, market research is more important for you than it is for a big company. Big companies can afford to misjudge the market and experience a flop; you can't. But you don't have to invest big bucks in market research to evaluate your business idea. Your biggest investment will be in time and effort.

A simple and logical place to start your research is by bouncing your idea off your friends and family, as long as you realize that they may not always be completely honest with you. Not that they mean to deceive you, but their feedback could easily be biased. Many of your friends will want to be supportive, and they won't want to pour cold water on your dream. Others may have a hidden agenda, causing them to discourage you unfairly. Some people don't want to see others they know succeed, so they are quick to put down any new ideas. Or maybe they're simply negative types who automatically look at the glass as half empty. Because it's hard to know what someone's agenda might be, you'll also need to reach beyond your intimate circle to gain more objective opinions of your business concept.

Identify your target market, and talk to potential customers. You might think everyone would be potentially interested in your product or service, but in reality that's not going to be the case. So define who will be your most likely customers. Then, ask questions. Find out what they like about the similar products or services that are currently available. Ask open-ended questions so you can see whether there are any unsatisfied needs. Don't be satisfied with "yes" or "no," go for the why—and why not—behind their answers. If you identify any unmet needs, that opens the door for you to describe your offering and find out whether they would be interested, if it were available. And, if so, how much would they be willing to pay? Remember, you are going into business to make a profit, so price is critical.

Talk to potential vendors and suppliers. Because they work with businesses similar to what you're considering, they usually have a good sense of the market environment. Don't ask or expect them to divulge confidential information, but question them in general terms about what's currently available and whether or not customer needs appear to be satisfied.

Another research option is to conduct an informal focus group. Invite a number of people you respect to your home, to a restaurant, or to a borrowed conference room. Introduce your business concept and encourage free discussion and feedback. Keep an open mind and listen objectively to the comments being made. You aren't there to defend, persuade, or convince—just to listen and learn. If you don't think you can remain neutral during the discussion, you may want to ask someone else to facilitate.

An Alarming Idea

Linda Sosna, inventor of the Tag Alarm, an alarm system for purses, briefcases, and backpacks, added an important feature to her hand-made prototype as a result of feedback she got from focus groups. Someone suggested she add a panic button to the electronic device. So before she went into production, she was able to add that safety feature, which enhanced the overall product offering. Today, Sosna sells all over the world via her website, and the product has been featured on QVC. Sosna believes that the added feature enhanced her ability to succeed in the market.

Focus Groups

Sosna was willing to listen to the feedback she received from her focus group; but that isn't always the case. I was invited to be part of an informal advisory board for a friend who was developing an Internet site for women. The group she put together was impressive, and she made us all feel like VIPs. But it was clear that she didn't really want to hear our input. What she wanted was to "tell" us what she was going to do, and she wanted us to rubber-stamp it.

Having survived the early stages of an Internet start-up, I recognized the flaws in her business model immediately. Yet when some of us objectively tried to point out the realities of the market and how her failure to understand the nuances involved would be the kiss of death, she clearly didn't want to hear it. Sadly, she lost a lot of her own money, as well as that of a few other investors. In fact, some of the investors were friends, so she lost the friendships, too. The site never got off the ground. (More about family and friend funding later.)

With a focus group, you have to be prepared to listen to what you might not want to hear, because it could save you money and time in the end. It's one thing to consider feedback and decide against the recommendations; it's another to be closed off to even considering others' suggestions. Don't waste your time or resources (or anyone else's time) on conducting a focus group unless you plan to keep an open mind.

To put together a good focus group or advisory board, reach out to a diversified group of individuals. Make a list of some of the people you know who fit into any of the following categories:

- Business owner

- Financial manager

- Successful salesperson

- Technology expert

- Attorney

- Commercial real estate professional

- Marketing expert

- Vendor (related to your industry or business)

- E-commerce expert

- Retail connection

- Human resources professional

- Accountant

Electronic Research Tools

Social media provides unique opportunities to conduct almost real-time focus groups and obtain good feedback. By circulating your idea through social media you can learn a lot about what the market wants. Additionally, some social media sites offer polls, survey tools, and discussion areas where you can engage and measure your market's interest in your product or service offering. Of course, be careful about revealing proprietary information, as someone could steal your idea. (More about protecting your idea in Chapter 8: "Protecting Your Business, Your Ideas, and Yourself.")

Online surveys also provide an opportunity to gain insight into the viability of your business idea. A number of companies provide online survey tools, along with templates to assist you in developing a professional survey. Not only can you get a general idea of the market demand for your product or service, but you can also use the survey to develop your marketing strategy and define market opportunities in your business plan. The survey can be sent to your personal database of friends, colleagues, and business associates. And you may be able to ask them to share the survey with people on their business or personal databases, too.

Finally, the college-level marketing or business classes in your area may be willing to conduct a research study for your business as part of a class project. It's a win-win: The students get the experience and you get the information.

Final Thoughts for a Great Beginning

Defining, refining, and evaluating your business idea not only enhances your opportunity for success but also provides solid information with which you can begin to draft your business plan. The process of analyzing the viability, profitability, and sustainability of your business concept takes time, but it is better to spend this time now than to waste months or years pursuing a business idea that was doomed from the start. Alternatively, with this research in hand, you've made a major step forward in reaching your business goals.

CHAPTER 4

---

build a powerful
business strategy

*An entrepreneur tends to bite off a little more than he
can chew, hoping he'll quickly learn how to chew it.*

—Roy Ash, cofounder of Litton Industries

ROY ASH WAS right. Confident that they can figure it out as
they go along, most entrepreneurs and small-business owners
strike out on their own without taking the time to develop a business plan. If you take that approach rather than embracing the
process of developing a business plan, you may save a little time,
but I guarantee you'll make more mistakes—potentially costly
ones.

The Value of a Business Plan

Every business, large or small, needs a business plan. In fact, every book written on the subject of operating a small business stresses the importance of creating a business plan. What's missing, however, is the "why" behind the development of a plan. Most of the published materials you'll find on business planning outline what you need to include in the plan and how it should be presented. But it's one thing to follow an outline and fill in the blanks and quite another thing to understand both why you are providing all that information and how it is going to affect your business. In my opinion, unless you understand the "why" behind the plan, then filling in the blanks does nothing more than create busywork.

Too many business owners and entrepreneurs think business plans are needed only to attract investors or to get loans. That's simply not the case. The business plan is an integral part of your business operations.

Despite the many characteristics that distinguish different types of business owners—such as age, ethnic background, experience, gender, location, and industry—there is one thing that all successful business owners and entrepreneurs have in common, and that is a clear vision of where they want their businesses to go. They aren't afraid to start out by thinking big—and then laying the foundation to get there. Most small businesses don't fail because their owners are thinking too big; they fail or flounder because they weren't thinking big enough.

So before you're into the thick of running your business on a day-to-day basis, consider what it is you really want that business to be when it grows up. Once you get caught up in the daily grind, it's tough to find the time and energy to create the big vision; so, do that big-vision thinking now.

Where would you like your business to be in five years? What will it look like in ten years? What is it going to take to get to both of those places? What is your exit strategy? That is, what do you want to do with the business when you are ready to retire or move on to something else? Sell it? Pass it on to your heirs? I've known business owners who knew from the outset that they wanted to grow the business to a certain level and then sell it within 10 years. Not all of them reached their goals by their target dates; but with a clear vision, most of them came closer to meeting them than did the entrepreneurs who started without a big picture in mind. Having a clear vision will guide you in making the right business decisions throughout your journey. So, this is your chance to fast-forward to the end of the movie, or skip ahead to the last page of the book and create the ending before you write the story.

Think of it as if you're building a house. You wouldn't start building the house without knowing what you wanted it to look like. You need to know how many bedrooms you want and how many floors there'll be. You hire an architect to draw up blueprints for the builders to refer to as they construct the house. Those blueprints guide the construction and specify the methods and materials that meet building codes. Similarly, your business is also a huge investment of time and money: Why would you ever start building it without a plan that reflects what you want it to become?

Another benefit of starting with a big-picture vision for your business is that it's contagious. When you can see the direction in which your business is heading, you can share that vision with others, and then they, too, will begin to see and believe in your business idea. I met an out-of-work single mom recently who sold her car and her grandmother's jewelry to launch a new business venture. She told me that, in five years, her company is going to be a $50 million business. And I think she might be right. She has a business plan that outlines precisely how she expects to build to that level. Her vision and her enthusiasm have already attracted a few small investors and some national attention. As she noted, "If you can't see it and believe it, then no one else can." Honestly, I can't explain the reason for a business plan any better than that.

It may sound like I'm harping on the importance of vision, but trust me—it is a crucial step in building a successful business. In short, the difference between a business lacking a vision and one having a vision is clear: In one you are just creating a job for yourself (one that may or may not work out); in the other you are building a sustainable, successful business enterprise. It's a difference that, unfortunately, many promising start-ups ignore.

Building a Sustainable Business

More and more people today are working as freelancers, consul - tants, and independent contractors, and they refer to what they do as their own businesses. From a technical perspective, they are correct. They aren't W-2 employees, so they don't get a steady paycheck from an employer. But if they stop doing the lion's share of the work, their income stops, too. So, in reality, what they've created for themselves is a job, not a business.

A *business* is an entity that is bigger than one person alone. When you build a business, the business eventually becomes sustainable with or without your daily involvement. As one entrepreneur put it, "A sustainable business makes money for you while you sleep." Sounds pretty good, doesn't it?

Take a photographer as an example. There are photographers who build names for themselves and demand large sums of money for their work, based on their reputations. When someone hires them to do a job, they can't substitute someone else, because it is their personalized work that the person is buying. The same is often true for attorneys with solo or small practices. The clients have a relationship with the attorney, and they trust that attorney's work; they don't want someone else representing them. Both the photographer and the attorney are in the same situation: They *are* their businesses. As a result, it is very difficult, if not impossible, for them to sell their businesses to someone else.

However, a photographer who creates a business process that is not based solely on his or her particular talent, or an attorney who builds a team of associates or partners, does have a *business* and is much more likely down the road to be able to sell that business as a going concern.

There is nothing wrong with choosing to start an operation that simply provides an income stream for you. That is a personal choice. In fact, countless people today are creating their own "jobs" in order to generate income independently because there are few traditional jobs available. However, you need to understand the consequences of that choice so you can make an educated decision about how you want to build a sustainable organization. There are only so many hours in a day, and there's only so much one person can deliver. That setup limits your operation's growth. And what would happen if you got sick and couldn't work for a while?

When you build a *business* on the other hand, as I mentioned, it can continue with or without your involvement. Doing so requires that you "scale" the product or service you will deliver to the market. By that I mean you must create a system to deliver your product or service so that it can be taught to others and repeated consistently by others. Although it's likely that you'll be the only one doing the work in the early days, as the business grows, you can teach others to do it. That's an important distinction, and it is what separates a business from other types of operations.

When we launched SBTV.com, for example, I was the only on-camera talent. I wrote and produced the majority of the video content. And for the first few years, people told me I *was* the business—but I knew better. I never wanted the company to be dependent on me, because that meant that, without me, it could never become a going concern. And I wanted a clear exit strategy in place; I didn't want to be writing, producing, and reading from a teleprompter forever. I wanted a business that had *value*, so I could retire or go off to other entrepreneurial ventures—which, as I write this book, is what I am in the process of doing. Once you establish a business that can function successfully without you, you've created a valuable asset.

When you go into business on your own—become a small-business owner—you will work longer and harder than you've ever worked before. But in my opinion, having a business—not just a job—is a fine reward.

The Path to Sustainability

Teresa and Ian Miller spent 20-plus years in high-level corporate positions with major brands. Teresa was in the technology field and Ian, a Harvard MBA, worked in retail, finance, operations, and distribution. After testing their idea for a high-end pet products business, they decided to leave their paychecks and benefits packages behind and launch Treats Unleashed. While both of them felt they had worked diligently on behalf of their previous employers, they found themselves working many more hours once they were on their own.

"I found myself working from 6 a.m. to midnight to try to get things accomplished," Teresa said.

Ian added, "For the first six months to a year, you struggle to find a daily routine. When you work for a large corporation, you walk in and pretty much know what your day is going to look like. As an entrepreneur you never know how your day may play out. Things come up and you do something completely different the rest of the day or the week."

So, think about it carefully. As long as you are working crazy, long, stressful hours, don't you want something sustainable—

something of value that you can sell or pass on to your heirs? You deserve to have something to show for all your hard work. Think about that when you're getting started in your new business, so you can take the right steps to get to the ending you deserve.

Make Your Business Plan a Process, Not a Task

Procrastination is your enemy. That's the number one biggest obstacle to writing a business plan. Many small-business owners avoid writing a plan because they don't know how to do it. It seems to them an overwhelming, intimidating, insurmountable task.

Instead of looking at your business plan as a monstrous task hanging over your head, think of it as a process of discovery. Unless you decide to enter a business-plan competition, your plan isn't going to be judged, so don't think of it as an academic challenge. Rest easy. You don't need a business degree, and the plan doesn't need to be anything fancy. The key to writing a good business plan is just being sure it makes sense. If it makes sense, you've got a winner.

If you invest the effort to march through all the aspects involved in developing a plan, it will equip you to start off on the right track. And the experience of writing your business plan will prove invaluable, because you'll learn much about your business in the process, which will increase the odds of your success.

Planning, Not Plans

Few people can sit down and write a business plan in a matter of hours or days. It's a learning process, so tackle it one piece at a time. No one has all the answers in the beginning, and, in fact, it's helpful to learn what it is you don't know. By going through the process, you'll learn how much you *don't* know about the business you want to start.

And as you gather the critical information you need for the plan, you'll have "Aha!" moments. Things that can have a positive impact on your business will come to light: Potential stumbling blocks may appear, and opportunities previously unseen may arise. Just keep an open mind and let the process of discovery guide you.

President Dwight D. Eisenhower once said, "Plans are nothing; planning is everything." It's really the process, not the business plan itself, that is important. Think about the process of creating a business plan as doing something that works *for* you, and not just as more work to be done. When you realize how important the process is for the success of your business, it becomes something you *want* to do—and do the right way.

An Ongoing Plan

Here's a question I received from a guest on one of my talk shows: "I wrote a business plan for my company over two years ago, basically to create some structure to follow. We launched the site September 2009. I have been bootstrapping this venture with my own funds, which are now nearly exhausted. The new ideas I have require a bit more capital. So, how do you approach writing a 'build onto' business plan since my company already exists?"

This question represents the way many small-business owners view their plans. They write them, then they set them aside and check that "detail" off their lists. That's a mistake. You've written your business plan, but you're not finished. Oh, no. The first business plan you write is just the beginning. Your plan will evolve over time as you and your business mature. Business plans have been referred to as "water for a thirsty plant." They keep businesses alive and thriving. Your business plan should be an ongoing part of your business process. You should refer to it regularly and make adjustments as needed.

The initial business plans I wrote for some of my start-ups looked pretty naïve as the businesses grew. What I thought would work early on wasn't always on target, so as the business matured so did the strategic direction of my business plan. However, the plan gave me a basis from which to start. It provided direction and established goals and measurements. In many respects, the business plan becomes an operating tool for your business. Without these fundamentals, you are flying by the seat of your pants. And while that lack of focus may work for a while, it's how a lot of businesses crash and burn.

Content Trumps Format

New entrepreneurs can get hung up on the format for their business plan. If they don't have strong backgrounds in business, they tend to be intimidated by the formats of standard plans and all the seemingly technical business projections that need to be included.

Don't be intimidated. I'm repeating myself, but I want to emphasize that you don't need an MBA to write an outstanding business plan. It's the *substance* of the plan that's important, and content trumps format every time. The more succinct your plan is, the better. A plan that rambles on for 50 to 100 pages is evidence of someone who lacks a clear understanding of what his business proposition is and how his business is going to make money.

A banker once told me about a meeting he had with a man who wanted a loan for his business. When the banker asked to see his business plan, the man said he didn't have one, so the banker told him to come back when he did. The man left and returned later with a business plan written on a brown paper grocery bag. The banker said it was the best business plan he'd ever read, and the man got the money he needed. That's because the business owner knew how to describe the business opportunity and define exactly what it would need to succeed. Content trumps format.

A brown paper bag may not be your style, of course. There are excellent resources on the Internet to help you write a business plan in a more standard format. Simply do a search for "business plans" and you'll find templates, articles, and software packages. My recommendation is the Palo Alto Business Plan Pro, which was developed by Tim Berry, author of *The Book on Business Planning*. In the spirit of full disclosure, I must tell you I am a personal friend of Tim's, and I blog on his company's website. But I have yet to find a program that is as user-friendly as this planning software.

Another great resource for help with your business plan is a Small Business Development Center. These centers are located around the country, and they offer assistance for start-up businesses. You can find a nearby location by going to www.asbdc-us.org. Additionally, many local economic development offices provide training and technical assistance for new and growing small businesses.

Some business owners outsource the development of their business plans to a company or individual who specializes in this activity. But unless you are hoping to raise millions in equity capital (i.e., from institutional investors), be careful about hiring someone else to write your plan. Institutional investors often require plans to be presented in a more formal structure. First, these services aren't cheap. Second, you are the one who is going to have to execute the plan, so you really need to understand it and be intimately involved in its development. If someone else writes your plan for you, what will you have learned from it? Without going through the process yourself, how will you acquire the knowledge you'll need to be successful? Third, how will you be equipped to modify the plan as adjustments need to be made? Most of the time, plans-for-hire go into a drawer and are never looked at again.

I made the mistake of using one of those services when I was seeking venture capital. The plan the service developed was so complex that it was impossible to print out all the spreadsheets without using a special printer. And I needed a weightlifter to carry them around for me. Plus, only someone with an advanced finance degree could possibly understand all the information. I spent many hours going over and over the plan. But it didn't take me long to realize that if I, the CEO of the company, couldn't explain the plan, I couldn't expect investors to believe in my ability to deliver results. Finally I created a "cheat sheet" that I could use for presentations. It may not have been as fancy as the one the service had created for me, but at least it was easy to understand: It showed how the company could use the funds I was seeking to achieve my goals and provide a substantial return on investment.

As painful as it may seem, the planning process will teach you more about your new business venture than you could possibly imagine. I guarantee it. So hang in there. Your efforts will be rewarded with a much greater chance of success.

What Do You Include in a Business Plan?

In addition to being an entrepreneur, I'm also a journalist, so I think of a business plan as something that answers the questions every cub reporter learns to ask: Who? What? When? Where? How? and Why? If you can answer all of these questions about every aspect of your business, you've got it made. What is your business? Where will you sell your product/service? Who are your customers? How, where, and why do they buy? How much money do you need? How much money can you make? Why are you the best person to build the business? Why is there a need for the business? Et cetera.

A business plan covers everything from explaining the nature of your business to outlining its financial projections. The key elements are:

• *Executive Summary.* This is the most important section of your business plan. The executive summary is a concise overview of the plan along with a description of your company. Even though it's presented at the beginning of the business plan, don't try to write the executive summary until after you have completed the rest of the plan. (It is, of course, impossible to write a "summary" of the plan until you know what is in the plan as a whole.) The executive summary is critical, particularly if you are looking for investment capital or debt financing. Often it is the only part of the plan that investors or creditors will read, so it needs to highlight the key elements of the plan.

• *Market Analysis.* This section illustrates your knowledge of the industry. It should also present general highlights of and conclusions from any market research data you have collected. (The details of your marketing research studies belong in the appendix section of your business plan.)

• *Company Description.* This section is a general overview of how the different elements of your business will fit together. It includes information about the nature of your business and the primary factors that you believe will make it a success. This is the section where you define the real value your business will bring to the market.

• *Organization and Management.* This section describes your company's organizational structure, details the ownership of the company, profiles the management team, and provides the qualifications of the board of directors if you choose to have one. (In small companies, typically the board and the management team are one and the same.)

• *Marketing and Sales Strategies.* Marketing is the process of creating customers, and customers are the lifeblood of any business. In this section you define your marketing strategy. There is no single approach to a marketing strategy; the strategy should be derived from an ongoing self-evaluation process that's unique to your company—and include the steps you will take to follow the strategy. (Chapter 6 contains the information you'll need to create a marketing plan.)

• *Service or Product Line.* What are you selling? This section describes your service or product, emphasizing its benefits to potential and current customers. Here, you give the big picture. For example, you don't specify which 89 foods you will carry in your "Gourmet to Go" shop; instead, you explain why busy, two-career couples will prefer shopping in a service-oriented store that records clients' food preferences and caters even the smallest parties on short notice.

• *Funding Needs.* This section includes estimates of your start-up costs and your ongoing capital requirements. If you're seeking outside capital, then you must include a funding request. Be specific regarding exactly how you plan to use the funds to grow your business. Failing to define funding needs clearly is a costly mistake that many small-business owners make.

• *Financials.* In this section you make projections about your company's future financial performance. The Palo Alto software program I noted earlier—Business Plan Pro—contains formulated spreadsheets to help you with the development of your financials. No need to worry about being a financial whiz kid.

Words of Wisdom

Because there is so much information readily available on the mechanics of preparing a business plan, I plan to focus on the "why" behind the information you need to provide. Once you understand how and why that information is used toward the development of your business, the process of creating the plan becomes easier. So I've put together a list of tips to keep you focused on your "why" and assist you in creating your plan.

1. Don't inflate your idea. It is always better to underpromise and overdeliver, even to yourself. So don't kid yourself by making your business plan look larger than life. Be realistic with the opportunity you see and the numbers you project. Remember, once the plan is written, you have to deliver those results.

2. Don't underestimate your start-up costs. A key reason many small firms fail is that they were undercapitalized. Trust me: It always takes more money than you think it's going to take to get your business off the ground. So give yourself a cushion. Also, don't forget about your personal income needs. Businesses don't make money from the first day of operations; it may take several years before you are able to draw a fair salary. You have to be prepared for lean years. As one seasoned entrepreneur noted, "If you are in business for 25 years, plan to lose money in at least seven of those years."

3. Don't overestimate how quickly you can grow the business. Zealous start-ups think they can set the world on fire, so they make growth projections that are unrealistic. Even if you're confident that you can build revenue quickly, create a worst-case scenario and plan accordingly. Typically, business owners find it takes two to three times longer than they estimated to build their businesses. If your plan is built on inflated projections, your business will suffer significantly.

4. Don't underestimate the competition. Many start-ups fail to properly assess the competition. It's essential that you understand the competitive landscape. Your plan must provide a comprehensive analysis of your competition and how your business will stand out from the crowd. Don't lull yourself into believing the product or service you're offering is unique. And even when there's no direct competitor for your product or service, customers and clients have other ways and preferences for spending money. Business is all about getting customers to reallocate their limited resources in your direction, so there will always be some competing forces.

5. Be specific and thorough. If you take a naïve or vague approach to your business plan, it will be a disaster. So many business plans are filled with vague descriptions instead of solid, defensible information; those plans have no value to anyone. Do the hard work to dig out the facts and make the plan a truly compelling demonstration of the viability of your business.

Your Elevator Pitch

When I write a business plan, I consider how I could sell that business concept in less than 90 seconds—which is known in the world of sales as an "elevator pitch." If you can craft a concise and catchy pitch that captures the attention of your audience, you should be able to build your business plan.

An elevator pitch has to be concise. (As the name suggests, you can't ramble on because there's not much time between floors.) And it should be easy to understand. Don't use words that the average person won't recognize.

Your pitch should get the listener to visualize your business and understand immediately how he or she could profit from it. Stories are powerful tools, so if you can quickly use a story to show how your business will work, you will engage the listener. And, as with any sales pitch, the best elevator pitch is one that's targeted to its audience, so know who your target customers are and what motivates their buying decisions. At the end of the pitch, if you've done a good job, the listener will be eager to learn more.

It's impossible to write a strong elevator pitch without first having done the necessary background work, as explored in your business plan. You need to have an intimate understanding of what your business is, who your customer is, what makes your business unique, and what your value proposition is.

The Most Important Part

Here's the harsh reality: If you can't demonstrate how you're going to make money in your business, then you are quite simply wasting your time. It's like walking down the aisle to marry someone when you know things aren't quite right and thinking that once you're married, you'll be able to fix it. Believe me, having gone through an unfortunate first marriage, I can tell you that early doubts don't get resolved. Problems only get amplified.

Like marriage, like business. You need confidence in the viability of your business before you open the doors. I've spent several of these early chapters in this book delving into personality and motivation, as well as personal financial situations. I've tried to shed light on the realities of the small-business lifestyle. I've shown you how to evaluate your business idea and how to begin defining your business strategy. Now you are at the critical point where you need to decide whether your business idea is going to pay off. Once you've made your decision—assuming it's positive—then proceed with it. Inaction is a decision in and of itself, and that may be your sign *not* to move ahead. But if you are ready, move on to Part II of this book for more tactical planning steps toward building a successful small business.

PART II

open for business
the strategic and tactical keys to business success

Developing a vision and creating a business plan are the first steps in the process of building a successful small business. The next steps involve determining the strategy and tactics that you'll need to make your vision a reality. The following chapters help you lay the foundation for making your small business a success. These key steps are derived not only from my own personal experience but also from having worked with many small businesses in a great many fields.

The key steps I describe here are based on what I call the "cornerstones of your business": purpose, promise, and principles. Upon this foundation, you construct the framework of marketing and sales, human resources, support services, location, pricing, and financing. These are what I'm calling the seven P's of business success—people, promotion, place, protection, pricing, process, and pennies. Part II concludes with some practical advice from someone who's been in the trenches and risen to success.

CHAPTER 5

purpose, promise, and principles
the cornerstones of your business

IN PART I, I TALKED about the importance of having a "big-picture" view of your business. Part of this "big picture" should be your business purpose. Why are you doing what you're doing? It's amazing how many business owners and their teams go through the motions of running their businesses on a day-to-day basis without ever understanding the purpose behind what they're doing. They might as well be zombies. Businesses without a purpose don't have a heart. They don't stand for anything, and as a result, they don't stand out from similar businesses. Successful business owners both understand their purpose and can articulate that purpose to their team, their customers, their investors—and in fact, to the world.

What's Your Purpose?

Think about the business brands you love. Don't you have a visceral understanding of their purpose? Consider the nearly cultlike following that Apple products have. People identify with the brand because it stands for something: innovation, efficiency, quality. It speaks to them.

It should go without saying that part of your business purpose is to make money. But making money shouldn't be the sole purpose of your business. There has to be a sense that the service or product your business provides brings value to the market, and that because of that value, the company makes money. A business that exists for the sole purpose of making money won't ever become a great business. Customers don't come to you because they want to make you rich. They come to you because they believe in the value you provide for them, whether that value is in detailing their car, grooming their dog, creating their estate plan, or selling them a lawn mower. So it's up to you to determine what that value is—that's your business's purpose.

You and everyone on your team needs to know that purpose. Even if you don't have a "team" yet, you should be able to answer these simple questions without hesitation:

- Why are we doing what we do?

- What purpose does it serve?

If you cannot explain your purpose to the marketplace in a story that motivates customers or clients to do business with you, then you will not succeed. You may manage to keep the doors open, but you won't soar to great heights. The same is true for your eventual employees, whenever you start to hire them. What motivates them to come to work each day? Loyal employees are motivated by more than just a paycheck. Your team needs to be fully engaged. Each should understand the role he or she plays, because everyone needs to feel part of the company's purpose—its heart and soul.

When business founders and their teams understand the business's purpose and vision, they project an energy that's exciting to all. I'm sure you've walked into businesses that feel, well, blah—flat, with no life. Such businesses go from project to project with no purpose other than making sure they make money on the deal. Then there are businesses that have an upbeat, energetic, focused atmosphere—and it's contagious. It makes you, the customer or client, feel good about doing business with this group.

For me personally, knowing the purpose of my business is extremely important for another practical reason: It drives me and gives me the courage and confidence to "sell" my company.

I've never liked or wanted to be in sales. In fact, I tried a couple of sales positions during my professional career, and, well, let's just say I didn't set the world on fire. Yet everyone tells me I'm a master when it comes to selling my own business. The reason has to be that I don't feel as though I'm selling, because I truly believe in what I'm doing and why I'm doing it. In fact, someone commented to me recently, "You don't do it for the money, do you?" Of course, I like—make that *love*—making money, but I am equally driven by my purpose. That is, I also love the excitement of doing something I feel is rewarding for the customer, as well as for my business.

Live It Like It's Today

If your business is in the planning stages, whatever your business purpose and big picture may be, you need to begin living as if they exist today. It isn't just a remote possibility or something you merely wish for; *it's going to happen.* By living it as if it already exists, you'll begin to see opportunities and take actions that fit appropriately with your business vision and purpose. Furthermore, by using stories and language to describe your business venture in a clear, positive, confident manner, you are in many respects helping to make it a reality.

Back in the '70s and '80s, books on "dressing for success" were popular. That's when "image experts" began recommending that people dress for the job they *want* to have, regardless of their current positions. You should use that same strategy when it comes to building your business. Present yourself and your business as if you have already reached your goal. The attitude and image you project today can help bring you to the next level.

You may have heard people say, "Fake it until you make it." Clearly, there is some truth to that. Of course, don't ever misrepresent yourself or your business. But look and act the part and it will help you become what you want to be.

Purpose, Meet Mission Statement

Writing a mission statement for the business is a task many business owners don't take seriously—and that's a big mistake. Your mission statement is the foundation of your company. It's the voice of your brand. It formally answers the question we discussed earlier: "Why do we exist?" Additionally, it demonstrates that you are making a promise to your stakeholders (e.g., your customers, employees, and the community).

Here are some of my favorite mission statements as of this writing, which expertly define the business purpose of each company:

Mary Kay Cosmetics: "To give unlimited opportunity to women."

Wal-Mart: "Saving People Money So They Can Live Better."

Walt Disney: "To make people happy."

Each company's mission statement both articulates the business purpose and makes a promise. Remember that the promise you make to your customers is something you should never take lightly. It should incorporate the core values of your operations and serve as the cornerstone of your organization's culture.

Don't confuse core values with marketing slogans. For example, "We are the number one customer service company" is a slogan, and not representative of an organization's core values. Thus, if you look at Walt Disney's core values, they expand on the intrinsic promise in their mission statement:

Three core principles help guide our daily decisions and actions:

- Act and create in an ethical manner, and consider the consequences of our decisions.

- Champion the happiness and well-being of kids, parents, and families in our endeavors.

- Inspire kids, parents, employees and communities to make a lasting, positive change in the world.[1]

In short, your business success will be integrally connected to the strength of your core values and business beliefs. Business is all about relationships built on trust and integrity. Your core values are important because they reveal what is of paramount importance to you. They are the promises—to your employees, clients, investors, and community—that you must be ready to live up to.

You Are Part of the Promise and Purpose

Why *you?* Because it is nearly impossible to separate the business owner from the business, especially in the early days of any business operation. You are an integral part of the vision, mission, purpose, and promise of your business. So you need to be able to answer the question: *Why am I the best person to build this business?*

When you write your business plan, you'll need to include information about your own managerial experience and background, along with those of any others who will be involved in the business. Many people assume that all that's necessary and expected is to include a standard résumé. However, your business plan will be stronger if you use this opportunity to really sell yourself. Selling yourself is especially important if you are presenting your plan or business idea in person.

Customers, clients, and potential investors will all want to do business with people they believe are winners. But how do they make that determination? It comes when they gain confidence in your ability to do what you say you will do. If it appears that you don't believe in your own abilities, they won't either. If you're shy about telling others why they should believe in your ability to deliver, don't expect them to feel comfortable betting on you and your business. Building a successful business requires an incredible amount of self-confidence. Answering the question "Why you?" will give you the opportunity to toot your own horn.

Stand by Your Personal Values

Your personal values must align with your business values. You must walk the talk. Sometimes that means walking away from a cash-rich opportunity because it doesn't align with your personal and business values. Though this is not an easy choice to make when you are trying to build a business, it is absolutely essential.

My three most important business and personal values are professionalism, respect, and integrity. And those values have been tested over the years. However, as difficult as it has been at times, I have remained steadfast to my values, and it has always turned out to be the best decision in the long run.

Let me share one such example. In 2003, I was awarded a contract to serve as the spokeswoman for a small-business program being sponsored around the country by a major national brand. The scope of the work required that I take on additional staffing, that there would be extensive travel on my part, and that I would have to decline a number of other opportunities. (This is what is known as the *opportunity cost*, which many entrepreneurs don't take into account. Every time you consider taking on a new project or taking your business in a new direction, you need to calculate the cost of losing the business you won't be able to manage or the deals you may have to forgo as a result of your decision.)

Soon after the contract was signed, there was a change in management, and I found myself working with new people who had a new set of rules and expectations. That alone was problematic. But the situation was further complicated by the fact that I was closely associated with the old team. If you've ever worked in a large organization, you know how brutal office politics can be. Even though I was an independent contractor, I was caught in the turmoil. Nonetheless, I was hopeful that tensions would subside and the project would move forward.

Then, I met "the man." He was an independent contractor like myself, and he had been assigned the role of project manager. In truth, he was one of the most abusive, unprofessional, unethical, mean-spirited individuals I'd ever met. (Now ask me what I really think about him.) He would call me in the wee hours of the morning and scream at me. He lied and degraded me in front of others. Soon, his behavior started making me physically ill. I realized I didn't have the stamina or desire to fight someone of his nature, nor did I want to be involved any longer with such a toxic human being. So I decided to take control of "me."

I called my primary contact at the big-name company and explained that my personal values of respect, integrity, and professionalism had been egregiously violated by "the man." I respectfully withdrew from the contract and wished the company much success with the project. He tried to talk me out of my decision, but I held my ground. And when I hung up the phone, I felt empowered. A lot of people thought I was nuts for having walked away from such a lucrative contract, but I knew it was the right thing for me to do.

As it turned out, two weeks later the opportunity to purchase the domain name SBTV.com appeared. I saw the big-picture chance for a new business I could create that had endless possibilities. If I had compromised my principles and remained with that project just for the money, I would never have had the chance to build the award-winning, multimillion-dollar company that SBTV.com became.

In the early days of your business it may be hard to remain committed to your purpose, promise, and principles, but remember that they are important ingredients for your ultimate success. When you compromise those principles, chances are you'll pay a significant price.

Forgive me for using this cliché, but my mother always said, "When God shuts a door somewhere He has opened a window. You simply have to turn around and look for it." There is too much opportunity in this world to compromise who you are and the values and principles for which your business stands.

Note

1. In March 2011, Disney published its second Corporate Citizenship Report, detailing its approach and progress in these areas for its fiscal year 2010.

CHAPTER 6

marketing and sales strategy

Many a small thing has been made large by the right kind of advertising.

—Mark Twain

EVERY BUSINESS needs a strategy to identify and reach customers, and to get those customers to buy its product or service. That's why your business plan must include a section devoted to marketing and sales strategy. This is where you define the market opportunity and describe who your customers are, how you are going to reach them, what you are going to charge them for your product or service, and how you are going to convince them to choose your business over a competitor's operation.

Who Are Your Customers?

In the last chapter I discussed business purpose and core values. Your answer to that initial question—*What's your purpose?*—will help you define your target customer.

Keep in mind that your business can't be all things to all people. No matter how broad you consider the appeal of your product or service, not everyone will be interested in it. That's why it's important to identify the appropriate *niche* for your business—your "sweet spot," as some people say. This identity will serve as the foundation for all your marketing strategies. Always keeping that niche in mind will prevent you from making costly mistakes.

When you did the research for your business plan, you defined the market opportunity. Now, as you begin to develop your marketing strategy, start with that global overview of your market. How large is the industry, and what are the current trends? For example, the American Pet Products Association said that, in 2010, Americans were projected to spend about $47 billion on their beloved companions. And it was anticipated that the pet industry would grow at about $2 billion annually. Those projections demonstrate a strong industry, and that should bode well for you if you're venturing into pet-related products or services.

Once you have reviewed the industry information, whittle down the numbers to determine how much of that market you might be able to capture. Your target market consists of the customers you believe are most likely to buy *your* particular product or service. For example, your ideal customer or client may be a dual-income family with a household income of over $100,000, two children, and either one or two pets. Utilizing census bureau information or other reference material, you should be able to estimate the number of families in your area that fit that description. Once again, understating your market opportunity is always better than overestimating it.

You can search online to find industry data, and trade associations are helpful as well. Here are some sources of useful information. (Also see the Appendix at the end of this book.)

- Research companies such as Dun & Bradstreet, Standard & Poor's Investor Services, and the Risk Management Association; all publish directories and industry surveys.

- FedStats (www.Fedstats.gov) is a website that provides statistics from more than 100 agencies.

- The U.S. Department of Commerce (www.doc.gov) provides demographic statistics on American families.

- Your local Chamber of Commerce and economic development council should have helpful demographic information for your local region.

- Small Business Development Centers (SBDCs) are an excellent resource to assist you in defining your potential target market. The SBDCs are affiliated with the U.S. Small Business Administration. They have access to both federal and local demographic statistical information.

What's in a Name? Everything.

Your company name is part of your business brand. The right name can help you attract business, while the wrong name may hinder your growth. So, it is worth your time and effort to think about a name that is not just a name, but that is also an integral part of your marketing strategy.

Unless you're a licensed professional and your name *is* your business (e.g., a CPA, attorney, or doctor), you may want to avoid using just your name as your business name. For example, in my late twenties, I owned a small boutique public relations and advertising firm, which I named Wilson & Associates. It wasn't the best name—certainly not very creative for that type of business, and it didn't explain anything about what I did. On the other hand, when I practiced law as a solo practitioner, using my name made sense.

To find the right name for your new business, start by making a list of all the valuable things your company offers, including intangibles such as good customer service, fast delivery, and other attributes. Then have some fun. Play around with words and ideas that relate to those concepts. Invite others to get involved, too. Sometimes people who aren't as close to your business idea can do a better job thinking up names than you can.

One of my companies is Susan-Says.® When I launched the company, I was focused on writing books and doing public speaking to inspire and help women to succeed in business. I was also teaching a women's entrepreneurial training course at the local community college. So I took the opportunity to use my new business as a case study for the class on creating a name. "Susan-Says" is the result of one class member's saying "It should be 'Susan Says' because women have done what Simon says all these years, and it's time to do what Susan says." And that was that.

But generally speaking, avoid being too cute or clever, because humor doesn't always translate well. While you may think the name is catchy, someone else—perhaps your potential customer—may not get it. Also, be careful not to infringe on someone else's business name. That can be a costly mistake. Check with your secretary of state's office and the U.S. Patent and Trademark Office online (www.uspto.gov) to see whether the name is already taken. Even if the name is available, make sure it isn't too similar to one of your competitors' names. You don't want to create confusion or have a customer who is looking for your business go to a competitor by mistake.

Generally, it's best to avoid geographic identifiers in your business name unless you're sure you will never do business outside your immediate area. The exception would be adding a geo-graphic location when conveying something positive about the product, as in some brand-name wines, coffee, and so on. For example, Panera Bread, a chain of bakery cafes, was founded in St. Louis, Missouri, and was originally known as The St. Louis Bread Company. When the chain began to expand through franchising, the name was changed to be better suited for other parts of the country. So, in choosing a name, you need to consider possible future geographic expansion. And keep in mind that when doing business on the Internet, you'll want a name that potentially works across the country and around the globe.

You should also avoid an alphabet-soup name. The government has enough of those—acronyms for agencies and programs: SBA, DOL, CCR, NAIC, OSDBU, and so on. Letters are difficult for people to remember, so be cautious in using initials in your busi-ness name.

As you're naming your business, think about a tagline you might use as well, and make sure the business name integrates well with it. And by all means, keep the business name short and simple; make it easy for people to remember.

Because every small business today needs a strong Internet pres-ence, when you've narrowed down your list of names, check to see whether the domain is available. It's important for your domain to closely resemble your business name because, again, it makes it eas-ier for people to remember your URL. Also, avoid using hyphens and domain endings such as .net, .biz, and .us. If you're worried that someone else will hijack your business name by taking one of those, then go ahead and register it, but a .com is the preferable domain ending for a business. And the advice about keeping your business name short and simple applies to your domain address as well. Lengthy business names and complicated domains are difficult for your customers to remember.

Naming your business can be lots of fun, but be sure to take it seriously, too. Once you've named your business, it's hard to change it down the road. It's not impossible, but it is difficult.

How Will Customers Find You?

Identifying the right marketing tools to reach your target customers is a challenge for every small-business owner. While going through all the critical steps to get to the point where they can open for business, many owners don't think ahead about how they're going to get customers or clients to come through the door. It's not as simple as announcing to the world that you're open for business. Initially, a few people may trickle in, but how will you drive the volume of business you need to be successful?

That requires a marketing plan. The big questions for a start-up business—or really for any small business—regarding marketing are: Where do you find the money to market your business? How do you know which are the best tools to use?

Here's my advice on marketing strategy. Use the "MACS" principle: massive amounts of common sense. By using common sense and taking advantage of the excellent, inexpensive marketing tools available today, a small business can build considerable brand buzz and ramp up its revenues.

Understanding the Marketing Basics

"Marketing" is an umbrella term that covers a wide range of functions, including sales, branding, public relations, brochures, logo development, direct mail, advertising, Internet strategy, newsletters, and merchandising (i.e., promotional products such as coffee mugs, pens, and magnets). Marketing is so complex that unless you're a marketing professional it's impossible to understand all the nuances involved with each discipline. As your business grows, you can work with a marketing professional to develop appropriate strategies for your brand development; but initially, there's much you can accomplish on your own.

Once you know who your target customers are, you can focus on strategies to best reach them. Mass media outlets such as radio, television, and newspaper advertisements are rarely the appropriate answer for a start-up. Why? For one thing, they are expensive. And then, you're paying to reach a lot of people who in most cases will never be interested in buying your product or service, and that's wasteful. Remember: *massive amounts of common sense!*

Unfortunately, many new business owners get lured into believing they have to make a big splash with their marketing in order to get the word out. Entrepreneurs frequently email me wanting to know how to get capital so they can run a television campaign, which they believe will solve all their marketing problems. Before they know it, they've invested a load of money, and yet they either have nothing to show for it or they're not equipped to support the level of business this kind of advertising drives.

Some Early Missteps

You may remember the popular sock-puppet television ads for Pets.com. The site was launched in February 1999, and it sold pet supplies to retail customers. Its high-profile marketing campaign featuring the sock puppet quickly made it a widely recognized brand. In fact, the sock-puppet spokesperson was interviewed by *People* magazine and appeared on *Good Morning America.* Unfortu - nately, the infrastructure of the business could not support the overwhelming attention and sales the marketing campaign drove. As a result, the company lost money and was out of business by November 2000.

Another great example is that of a wildly successful entrepreneur, E. Desmond Lee, a classmate, peer, and friend of Wal-Mart founder Sam Walton. Lee founded a company that manufactured trouser creasers in the late 1930s, and he eventually built the company into an international source for manufacturing and distributing closet organizing systems. But in the early days, Lee was an unsophisticated businessman, and with just one major misstep, he nearly put himself out of business.

"The head of an advertising agency came to us with the idea that we would have an artist create an advertisement showing a model hanging a pair of trousers on the clothes line to advertise the pants creaser. It was a full-page in color and was to run in *Better Homes and Gardens*, movie magazines, *Good Housekeeping*, and *Life*. The total cost was about $200,000," Lee explained.

At the time, the company's annual revenues amounted to no more than $300,000. Nonetheless, dreaming of the big time, Lee made the decision to undertake the national campaign. "We had three inquiries and we didn't sell a single item," he said. "We were strapped financially. We were out of cash to pay our employees. Plus, there were other unpaid bills. We were nearly broke."

Don't you go broke trying to reach customers. Here are the most important things to remember.

1. "Open for business" doesn't mean business will come.

2. Always focus on your target market.

3. Never create expectations you can't meet.

4. Bigger and more expensive doesn't necessarily mean better.

5. Don't let your ego drive your marketing decisions.

Focus on Substance, Not Sizzle

Your business brand comprises all aspects of your business, including your office location, your marketing materials, and your phone answering system. New entrepreneurs, particularly those who come from corporate environments, often get paralyzed by perfection. Even before they open their doors, they think they must have the "right" image—which, by inference, means expensive. They set up an elaborately decorated office space, design fancy marketing materials, and invest in an elaborate Internet presence before they open the doors.

Don't spend money on fluff. People often invest a lot of money in window dressing because that's the way things were done at their old, brand-name companies. That's not surprising because large corporate entities have correspondingly large budgets. But high cost isn't the only problem with this marketing fluff; such things take a great deal of time to complete. I frequently hear comments like, "I'll be ready as soon as I get my marketing brochures printed"; "Once I get the design finished . . . "; and "I'm waiting for my new logo." Excuses, excuses, excuses. Successful entrepreneurs are already out the door, bringing in the business.

You can't afford to make the mistake of doing things the way they were done when you were an employee at a large organization. The small-business lifestyle is all about bootstrapping—looking for ways to get things done quickly, professionally, and inexpensively. Entrepreneurs learn how to do a lot with very little.

The good news is that you don't need a big budget to look big. Technological advancements offer tremendous opportunities for small businesses to create a professional image without incurring significant costs. There are some types of businesses you can launch for as little as a few hundred dollars in start-up capital. Yet, I've seen some new business owners spend thousands on just a company website.

In today's business environment you can have champagne taste on a beer budget. For example, if you need office furniture, look for a store selling refurbished office furniture in your area. Many new business owners find used office equipment and furniture on sites such as eBay and Craigslist. One business owner I met bartered his services for the furniture, equipment, and marketing materials he needed to get his business started—about $200,000 in value.

Even if you have ample funds to invest in your business start-up, don't blow them all up front on window dressing. Set some aside for a rainy day. It is smart to maintain cash reserves for working capital so you don't find yourself in a cash-flow crunch.

Define Your Marketing Message—and Be Consistent

Before you start choosing your marketing tools, know what you want to say. What is your marketing message(s)? You may adjust your marketing message periodically, or you may have different messages for different audiences, but focus on something from the start and be consistent. Here are some guidelines that will serve you well:

• *Be concise.* You don't need to include everything there is to know about your business in your marketing materials. Go back and review the purpose, promise, principles, and core values you estab- lished for your new company. What makes you different from everyone else in the market? This will be an important part of your marketing message. Stand out from the crowd and give people a reason to patronize your business instead of a competitor.

• *Be consistent.* Don't confuse people with too many things, and don't change your message frequently. A simple consistent message is easier to remember. It takes time for your message to cut through the clutter and be heard. So if you want your message to resonate, you must repeat the same message time and time again.

• *Focus on the customer.* Always create marketing messages that feature the customer, rather than your product or service. It is what's commonly known as WIIFM—what's in it for me. For example, let's say you're a car salesperson and the car you're trying to sell is equipped with state-of-the-art antilock brakes that can keep you from having an accident. Instead of relating to your customer the technical features of the brake system, share a story. Obviously, the fact that brakes are a safety feature will appeal to your customer's concern for safety. So you could explain how your customer's family won't be at risk if there's a major snowstorm because of this car's state-of-the-art antilock brakes. See the difference?

As I noted earlier, your key messages may be different for different audiences. As the business owner and primary sales representative, you listen and learn what each audience wants and then align your message accordingly.

• *Deliver on your promises.* Never guarantee something in your marketing materials unless you are absolutely positive you can deliver on that promise every single time. Establishing expectations with your customers or clients and not living up to them will tarnish your reputation quickly. News of bad service and unfulfilled commitments travels fast.

Make sure all of your marketing messages match your actions. This is known as *brand integrity.* Many business brands make the terrible mistake of saying one thing in their marketing and doing something else when it comes to delivering their products or ser - vices. If your marketing campaign says that customer service is paramount, but you have people in your organization who ignore complaints or don't respond in a timely fashion, then you minimize the effectiveness of your marketing efforts. Again, walk the talk.

Select the Right Marketing Tools for Your Business

Smart business owners make sure their marketing dollars are directed to the right people. Are your potential customers involved in a certain type of community activity? Do they belong to a particular trade or professional association? Identify where, how, and when they consume information, and see to it that your message is there, too.

What focused marketing tools should you use to reach your customers? In the confines of this book it would be impossible to cover the endless marketing avenues available to a small business. Check the Appendix for more detailed assistance. Here, I'll highlight some resources I find most effective for the majority of small businesses.

Customer Interface

We aren't living in a nine-to-five world anymore. Americans are working longer hours than ever before, and look for services that match their schedules. Therefore, if you want to succeed in business you need to be available when your customers are most likely to want your services or products.

Don't set your business hours arbitrarily. You need to listen to your market. For example, I worked with a dentist who had been in practice for many years, yet was losing patients. He tried a variety of traditional marketing methods, including radio advertisements, but nothing seemed to turn the tide. I had suggested he get feedback from his patients, particularly those who had not scheduled an appointment in some time. So he created a survey and emailed it to his patient list.

What he learned startled him. His office wasn't open during the hours that were convenient for many of his patients. The dynamics of the business environment had shifted, but the dentist hadn't made appropriate adjustments. Worried about their job security, patients weren't willing to take time off to go to the dentist during a workday. And the dentist's office was open only one evening per week and one Saturday per month. In response to this information, the dentist changed his office hours. He opened three Saturdays each month and increased his evening hours significantly. As a result, his patients responded and his practice picked up.

It is up to *you* to make it easy for your customer or client base to do business with you. To succeed in a competitive environment, you must meet consumer demands. If you aren't there when customers want you, your competitor will be.

Internet Presence

If you're in business today and you don't have a website, you're just being plain stupid. The number of people who turn to the phonebook to find a business is rapidly shrinking. So, if for no other reason, you need a website so your customers can find you. If you aren't on the Internet, they will find someone who is. Think about all the smartphone applications that search for businesses, locate them, provide directions, share reviews, and link to the business website for more information. Once again, it's just MACS—*massive amounts of common sense.*

Thanks to technology, it's extremely affordable for a small business to create an Internet presence. The first website I developed for one of my businesses cost about $10,000, and it was a static online brochure that I couldn't manage myself. Today, there are myriad resources offering design templates, so even the most technologically challenged individual can create a site in a relatively short amount of time. Many of these resources include domain name registration and hosting services for free, or just a nominal monthly fee.

To make sure your site really works for your business, commit to adding fresh content on a regular basis. That is, give people a reason to come back to your site. For example, offer a tip of the day or week, or perhaps a weekly special or discount. You might profile one of your customers (with the individual's permission) as a case study. You can also spotlight a new product offering or provide some timely industry-related information.

Make your site as user-friendly as possible. Don't clutter it with numerous fancy fonts. People aren't interested in a complex display or clicking their way through a maze. They just want what they want when they want it. And this sounds really obvious, but be sure to provide a way for people to contact you. It's very frustrating when someone has a question and there is no "contact us" information.

You can also use your site to capture customer information and email addresses. The more you know about your customers, the better you can serve their needs. With a database of email addresses, you can develop communication programs that allow you to stay in touch and remain at the forefront of your customers' minds.

Post links to positive media coverage your company has received. This adds credibility to your business. If you are capturing emails on your site, you can also forward to news coverage links to your database.

Finally, your website should be mobile-friendly. Because customers today want everything at their fingertips, chances are they're accessing your site via their smartphones. Many refer to this as the golden age of the empowered consumer. The "Golden Entertainment and Media Outlook 2011–2015" from PricewaterhouseCoopers found that smartphones will account for 37 percent of online expenditures by 2015.

Public Relations

A television or radio interview. A magazine article. An Internet blog posting. All of these are opportunities that could help your business gain credibility and build awareness in the marketplace. In the past, it was expensive to hire a public relations firm to help a business attract media attention. Now there are simple ways in which you can turn your business into a media magnet, as I'll explain here.

Once again, it's important that you understand your message and define your objectives. In the past, it was common practice to distribute press releases everywhere you could—the old throw-the-spaghetti-against-the-wall-and-see-what-sticks approach. Not anymore. Just as you target your customers, you need to target the appropriate media. Identify the media outlets and specific journalists who cover stories pertaining to your industry or business. Pay attention to what they write about and how they cover the topics. How do you and your business connect with their interests and their audience? Then begin to develop a media contacts list.

When you're ready to reach out to a journalist or blogger, make sure what you're pitching has a newsworthy angle—and that it's not just an advertisement for your business. Whenever possible, tie your pitch to a current news story or a timely issue. At ItsYourBiz.com I get countless media pitches, even from PR professionals, who send information about a person or company and offer me their availability for an interview. There is a slim possibility that I might be working on a related story when that information lands in my in-box, but in most cases, I just hit the delete button. To be effective in attracting media attention, you need to find a news hook and help the journalist see the story angle.

For instance, become a media resource by subscribing to services such as Help a Reporter Out (www.helpareporter.com), which is free, or ProfNet, which charges a subscription fee. Journalists use these tools to submit queries pertaining to stories on which they're working. Some of the media outlets on these services are small, such as Internet radio programs, but there are reporters and producers from major outlets as well. Your success depends on knowing the appropriate way to respond to a query. Help the reporter understand why you are the best person to be interviewed. Provide several key bullet points that you are prepared to discuss in reference to the story. Bombarding the reporter with paragraph after paragraph of information will only cause him or her to delete your response immediately. Also, not providing enough information concerning the specifics you'll discuss regarding the topic will most likely knock you out of the running.

There are press-release distribution services you can use that make it easy for a small-business owner to manage the process and reach a host of media outlets. A well-written newsworthy release may be picked up and used in its entirety today because of reduced staffs at many media companies. To capture a reporter's attention, identify a problem to feature in the headline and then explain why your business is the solution. Provide credible information and advice that will be helpful to the audience.

Many local media sites offer places to post your press releases. Some of the free press-release services include Prweb.com, Prfriend.com, Free-press-release.com, Express-press-release.net/free, and eReleases .com. There are also subscription services, such as PRNewswire.com, dBusinessNews.com, and PitchEngine.com. The benefit of using a paid service is the additional SEO (search engine optimization) and tracking benefits you receive. After you've distributed the release, sign up for alerts from the various search engines, such as Google, so you'll know if someone picks it up.

It's helpful to establish an area on your site posting your news releases. Sometimes media sources will read current news releases in order to get background information on your business. Additionally, if you have used strategic key words when you posted them on your site, you may attract search-engine traffic.

Social Media

"Social media" is a broad term that encompasses everything from blogs and podcasts to community networking sites. Using social media gives you a platform to share information and be seen as an expert in your business field.

Small-business owners are rapidly embracing social media. About half of them say that they are leveraging social media to connect with their customers and increase their sales (though social media should rarely be used as a direct sales tool). Social media provides a unique way of communicating with your customers, almost in real time. You can disseminate messages, and your customers can also interact with you. You can also use social media platforms as a tool for listening to what the market is saying about your business—and what customers are saying about your competitors.

When Casey Ray decided to terminate his agreement with a dog-training franchise and start his business over again on his own, social media made the transition go smoothly. "Today, with tools like Facebook, you can reach 500 people all at one time and tell them you are changing your name. So it really went smoothly, but I can't imagine trying to do that without that type of media," explains Ray.

Similarly, James Berglie, of Be Photography, in Baltimore, has been using Facebook as a way of getting his work out to as many potential brides and grooms as possible. "Facebook has been a blessing. . . . Today, our clients see our photos from their friends' weddings as soon as they are ready, and they get to see all the work we do (even non-wedding-related) . . . and they continuously see our feed—they start imagining themselves in our shots. . . . They have been following us for the last one to two years, and know they want to use us before they even get engaged."

Social media sites are a potentially game-changing tool. It would be foolhardy for me to go through all the social media tools because, as rapidly as this landscape is changing, by the time you read this book there will be new resources, new tips, and different tricks. So here are some general guidelines to help you leverage these opportunities, regardless of the platform you choose:

1. To reap the benefits of social media, start with a plan and make a commitment. A halfhearted effort will result in extremely poor results. What is it you want social media to do for your business? Branding? Generate leads? Search for business partnership opportunities? Customer service? Feedback? Using social media can be successful for all these things, so establish a hierarchy of your primary, secondary, and tertiary goals.

2. As you begin to establish a social media presence, you'll need something to connect all the pieces. That connector should be your website and/or blog. It's like the center of a wheel, with each of your social media sites as spokes. By directing your social media efforts back to your website or blog, you can measure your results and begin to convert connections into leads, and ultimately, into customers.

3. Limit the time you spend on social media. One of the reasons many businesses don't embrace social media is that they think it will be too time-consuming. So start slowly with your social media efforts, and don't overwhelm yourself at first, because if you do you probably won't stick with this brand-building tool. Decide how much time you can allot each day or week, and then make that part of your to-do list. Don't try to be on all fronts at once. Choose the media you think will be most appropriate for your target audience; if you aren't sure, ask some of your customers which tools they use. Don't imagine your customers aren't involved in social media. As of this writing, if Facebook were its own country, it would have the fourth largest population in the world. Even my 86-year-old father has more than 100 Facebook friends!

4. Don't know what to say? Business owners frequently get asked questions about their businesses and their related industries. Use those questions as a way to begin a dialogue through social media. Share helpful articles or blog posts with your connections. Offer valuable tips and resources. Position yourself as a source of useful information. Remember, don't make "selling" your goal; make your goal building relationships that can turn into sales opportunities.

5. Use an aggregator. Aggregators connect all your social media profiles so you can input an update just once and it will post on multiple platforms, saving you a lot of time. (Currently, a few of the most popular aggregators are SocialOomph.com, Hootsuite.com, and TweetDeck.com.) These tools also allow you to schedule updates to go out periodically. But don't rely on them exclusively. Remember, the benefit of using social media is to interact with others and when you preschedule updates you minimize your opportunities for interaction.

6. Make your updates more than a one-way communication. Use social media to make communications and so engage people so they will respond to your updates, and comment on theirs as well. Don't worry about using some of the same material more than once. In many respects, social media sites are like 24-hour news services: Different people are logging on at different times of the day.

7. Online video is another effective social media resource and is an excellent medium for showcasing your product and/or service. In 2009, comScore found that 86 percent of U.S. Internet users view online video content every month. YouTube reports that there are about 24 hours of new video content uploaded on its site every minute. YouTube allows you to create your own channel, but you can also embed YouTube videos on your own website, which means you don't have to manage a video delivery platform on your website.

8. Whatever type of social media you decide you use, remember: Never post anything you wouldn't want the world to see. Even

if you think your privacy settings provide protection, you can't be too careful. An advertising agency representative lost his job because of one careless Tweet. He flew into a small city to meet with a major client, and upon landing, he sent a Tweet about how awful the town was. By the time he arrived at the client, upper management had already been apprised of his comment and he was asked to leave. In the fast-paced social media world, careless comments can be costly.

9. Protect your brand by establishing social media guidelines for your employees. It's also important to make clear what you consider acceptable and unacceptable in terms of employees' using social media for personal interests while at work. Remember that what your employees post online can reflect on your brand, and may also result in legal complications if they are found to injure a co-worker, competitor, or customer. Do an Internet search and you'll find social media tool kits created for employers; they provide important guidelines and information you need to know.

Other Marketing Means

Don't overlook some of the tried-and-true means for building a customer base. The following have been used by companies for years because they yield good results.

Coupons Make a Comeback

Historically, coupons were distributed by the manufacturers of packaged goods for use by consumers at various retail stores. They were widely distributed through newspapers, magazines, and other print media. These consumer brands sought means to reach the masses, but this type of widespread distribution was expensive. Today, couponing is enjoying a resurgence and is taking on a new, more targeted format. A.C. Nielsen, an independent marketing research firm, found that 95 percent of all shoppers like coupons and 60 percent actively look for them.

Offering coupons can help a small business attract new customers. It's also a clever strategy to entice inactive customers back to your business. But instead of purchasing ads and distributing printed coupons en masse, you can use technology to control costs and more effectively target your audience.

For example, post printable coupons on your website. Include a coupon in your e-newsletter or email marketing campaigns. Join a deal-of-the-day type coupon program, such as Groupon or similar local community programs. If you are a professional service provider, call the "coupon" a courtesy discount offering on a future service.

A quick word of caution about daily-deal coupons: While these companies can potentially generate a significant amount of business for you, they can also turn into a nightmare if you don't do your homework. Most of these distribution services take about 50 percent of the coupon price, which leaves very little for the business owner. So make sure you are at least covering your cost, and put limits on the offer, such as only one per customer. Be careful—if you aren't prepared to handle the potential influx of business, you could find your reputation ruined by negative online reviews and dissatisfied customers.

Finally, coupons are an excellent tool for generating return business. Before a customer checks out, provide a coupon as an enticement to come back. This works with both product and service businesses. Offer a 10 percent discount on a specific service upon the next visit, or a free product. My dog groomer gives me a coupon for a free nail clipping, tooth brushing service, or some type of discount after a certain number of visits, which of course gives me a reason to bring the dogs back again rather than trying a competitor.

Customer Loyalty Programs

No matter how small your business is, it never hurts to have a customer loyalty program. It's much less expensive to keep your existing customers than it is to attract new ones, so why not show your customers how much you appreciate their business? Customer loyalty programs can be structured in many ways, so just choose the strategy that works best for your type of business.

For instance, most programs are based on a point system that allows the customer to accumulate points based on frequency of purchase or dollar amount, which they can use for discounts or free products. Even if you have a service business, you can build a loyalty program. For example, if you are an IT consultant, a customer who reaches a certain level of business could get a free training class or some other type of support service.

The Belleville Farmer's Market, an Illinois-based community fresh produce market, designed an interesting loyalty program. They created a customer loyalty card that allows the consumer to select a charity to benefit from their purchases. Last year, this small family-owned business was able to donate $30,000 to local charitable organizations. Not only does the program give customers a reason to shop in the store, but many of the supported charities like to shop there as well to show their appreciation.

In addition to the charitable giving program, the Belleville Farmer's Market uses tech tools to build customer loyalty. For example, the store launched an email marketing campaign to build relationships with its customers. Starting with zero, the business built its database to more than 10,000. It uses twice-weekly emails to share special discounts and promotions with its customers.

Referrals—a Great Door Opener

Of course one of the best ways to build your business is to get referrals from your existing customers. Did you know that the majority of your customers would be happy to provide referrals if you did one simple thing? Ask. That's right; if you don't ask, you don't get. A customer referral is an excellent way to get your foot in the door with a new client or customer. It provides a stamp of approval, and people tend to rely on the opinions of others when it comes to making many of their buying decisions, both personally and professionally.

Some companies provide rewards for customer referrals in the form of discounts on services or products. Or, you could offer to make a donation in the customer's name to a charity of his or her choice. Social media can be used to get referrals as well. One of the leading Internet marketing research firms, eMarketer, found that 68 percent of U.S. Facebook users said they were more likely to buy because of a positive Facebook friend referral.

So make it a practice to ask.

Start Talking!

Do your knees shake and your palms sweat at the mere mention of speaking in public? There are many different groups and organizations looking for great speakers, so get over your fear and volunteer. Create an informative presentation related to your business and share your expertise.

Don't fret over the fact that you're not an experienced motivational speaker. The benefits are too great to miss. By appearing before a group, you'll gain credibility as an expert. And the chances of getting new customers from sharing your information are significant. Just don't make the mistake of doing an infomercial. (Not only will you face disgruntled audience members, but you'll never be given another chance.) Remember that the key to making a successful presentation is providing interesting and helpful information for your audience.

One of my favorite small-business vendors, Constant Contact, hosts seminars around the country on email marketing. These are not sales presentations; they are truly training seminars. Similarly, if you focus on educating your market, customers or clients will come to you as a credible and reliable resource.

The financial services industry is another example where educational seminars can pay huge dividends. Stockbrokers and investment counselors face fierce competition. Making sales call after sales call will eventually yield results, but it is time-consuming. Many successful investment counselors host seminars designed to inform potential investors about various investment strategies.

So use your speaking opportunites to position yourself as a subject-matter expert. If you're successful, you won't have to "sell." People will want to do business with you because you are *the* resource. But, again, if you try to turn your presentation into a sales pitch, your speaking career will be short-lived.

Networking the Old-Fashioned Way

Everyone talks about the importance of networking. Every motivational speaker, small-business expert, business coach, and self-help/business author will, at some point, include the boilerplate networking banter. It's become so common that I'm not sure anyone really understands what it means to network anymore.

Networking isn't a race to see how many business cards you can load into your database or how many friends you can add to your social media profile page. Real networking is about real people and real relationships—face-to-face interactions.

To reap the business rewards of networking, you must be committed. You aren't in the right mindset for networking if you're out for instant gratification. An effective network is built on a solid foundation of relationships acquired over time. When you make a new business acquaintance, take the time to learn as much about her or him as you possibly can. Don't look at the individual with dollar signs in your eyes. Take time to listen and learn by asking open-ended questions. A business acquaintance of mine always asks this, which is an excellent icebreaker: "So, tell me about yourself." Are there common interests you share? Do your children go to the same school? Remember, people do business with people they like—with friends.

Next on my list of best practices is to follow up after that initial meeting. Stacking the business cards on your desk or scanning them into Outlook doesn't create a network. Sending your new acquaintance a brochure or sales letter doesn't develop a relationship. And calling to set an appointment or make a sale won't do the trick, either. However, taking time to offer assistance and develop a relationship is what will ultimately build a solid network.

For example, let's say I meet you at an event, and during our conversation you mention you are a dog lover. Guess what? So am I. We have a nice conversation, and you tell me you'd like to know more about creating a dog-friendly office environment. So what do I do? I go back to my office and send a "Nice to meet you" email. But in addition, I include a link to an article with advice for pet-friendly workplaces.

Remember: Give, give, give. You know the adage "It's better to give than to receive." Nowhere is this more pertinent than in networking. Be willing to put the other person first. Find out how you can help the person and make sure to follow through. Perhaps you can make an introduction or suggest a good resource for the individual's business. Become the "go-to" person. Then, when *you* need assistance, you'll be abundantly rewarded.

There is no better asset—personally or professionally—than a strong network. A good friend describes it as putting it out to the universe—your universe; whether you need an excellent lawyer or a fabulous hair stylist, your network is the place you go.

Who Is Your Competition?

You can't effectively market your business until you understand your competition. What are their strengths and weaknesses? What's their pricing strategy? Who are their key customers? How can you differentiate yourself from them?

Over 66 percent of respondents to a survey conducted by the Society of Competitive Intelligence Professionals (SCIP) said that *competitive intelligence* is extremely or very effective in helping identify market opportunities. Nearly 44 percent found it extremely or very effective in terms of understanding customer demand. Nothing can be more disastrous for a small company than to be blindsided by a competitor's strategy.

Additionally, never make the mistake of assuming you don't have any direct competitors. Even if you have a brand-new type of product or service, you still have competition. Whether you sell to consumers or other businesses, there is only so much money to go around. You have to compete to get your target customers to choose to spend their money with you rather than with a competitor.

For example, ItsYourBiz.com (formerly SBTV.com) was the first—and continues to be the only—video news and information site for small businesses. When we started the business, video on the Internet was in its infancy, so we really didn't have any direct competition. However, because we depend almost exclusively on advertising revenue, we had competitors who were going after the same advertising dollars that we were. Companies have budgets, and they are going to divide those budgets among various suppliers. So we needed to establish a strategy that demonstrated why video content for small business was a better return on their investment than the primarily text content offered by others.

So how do you find the competitive information you need? Start the easy way—browse the Internet. Know what is on your competitor's website. What are their key selling messages? You may be able to discover pricing information on the site as well. There also could be information about new product launches or personnel changes. Press releases and news articles are also good sources of information. And don't forget about social media. You can monitor what is being said about your competition on various social media sites. Listen and learn. Personally, I use TweetDeck to monitor competitive activity, but there are other resources as well.

By using your social media tools, you can follow your competitors and see what they are promoting, and learn what customers are saying about them. If you discover a competitor's disgruntled customer, that's an opportunity to develop a lead.

Vendors are another good source of competitive information. Chances are one or more of your vendors also sells to your competitor. Your vendor may be able to give you some insight about what your competition is up to. But tread lightly. Remember, if the vendor willingly discloses information about competitors, most likely that vendor will also disclose information about you.

Track your competitors' advertisements. How are they positioning themselves? How often do they advertise? Where are they advertising? To whom are their ads directed? Collecting this information will help you get a better understanding of your competitor's overall strategy.

Secret shoppers can be a good way to learn about a retail competitor's sales process. Ask a friend or family member to pose as a potential customer and either call your competitor or visit their retail location. (Ethical business practices dictate that this wouldn't be appropriate in an industry where sales presentations are customized.)

In some cases you may even be able to talk directly with your competitors. Depending on what industry you are in, you may find your competitors are friendly and willing to discuss certain issues with you. The Society of Competitive Intelligence Professionals is a good resource for guidelines.

Finally, whatever information you obtain, use it constructively to assist your own firm's growth. Never use it to hurt your competitor. Not only does this make you look bad, but you could also run afoul of laws and regulations. And if you gain access to information that appears to be proprietary, destroy it immediately.

CHAPTER 7

---

people matter

PEOPLE CAN MAKE or break your business. That includes your professional advisers, suppliers, customers and clients, employees, business partners, and even your friends and family. Making wrong decisions about any of the people with whom you deal can significantly hurt your business and impede—even destroy—everything you are trying to achieve.

With regard to people, I've made both good calls and bad. In most cases, the bad calls were no big deal, but a few of the bad choices left me feeling angry and betrayed. There's an old saying: Business is business and friendship is friendship, but when it's your business, it's always personal. Fortunately, I've been able to rebound from bad calls, but not all entrepreneurs are so fortunate. Some find placing their trust in the wrong people to be too devastating, emotionally and financially, to overcome.

A Story of Betrayal

A number of years ago, I personally saw the tragic ending for a friend who simply couldn't overcome business betrayal. I'll call her Sally.

Sally had tremendous entrepreneurial drive. She built a business from nothing in 1993 to nearly $100 million in revenue by 2006. She recognized that she didn't have the sophistication to develop the structure and process for such a large organization, so to help her manage the rapid growth, she hired a chief operating officer. Things seemed to be going well until documents from the IRS arrived indicating she owed $2 million in back taxes.

A complicated investigation ensued, and it turned out that the trust Sally had invested in her second-in-command had been misplaced. According to sources close to Sally, the COO, who had previously been convicted of IRS fraud, failed to pay the company's federal taxes for two years. The IRS troubles caused other financial problems, too, putting the company in dire financial straits. Ultimately, Sally left her office one Thursday evening and never returned. Her body was found on Saturday. She had taken her own life. As one of Sally's friends noted, "Sally believed that she would lose herself if she lost her business. She had fought so hard for so many years to build that company, and she was deeply ashamed about her financial problems."

This is an extreme story. But I feel compelled to share it because it drives home the importance of understanding that your business is only as good as the people involved with it. Surround yourself with quality people, and be careful about where you place your trust. Every choice you make has an impact on your success. Oprah Winfrey has said that she continues to sign most of the checks in her business. Sage advice from a successful business owner.

The Fork in the Road

Thomas Edison had an unusual way of hiring his engineers. He'd hold up a lightbulb and ask the candidate how much water it would hold. Some candidates used gauges, measurements, and scientific calculations to determine the answer. Others simply filled the bulb with water and then poured the contents into a measuring cup. Which candidates got the job? The ones who used the simple approach—filling the bulb with water. Develop an "Edison Test" for your business.

Small businesses often start out as one-man or one-woman shows. As the owner, you do everything from collecting the cash to emptying the trash. As your business grows, however, it can reach a point where the volume of work for one person becomes overwhelming. In terms of the success of the business, that's not a bad thing, but it can cause you great stress and put you at risk for burnout. With only so many hours in a day, there are limits to what one person can accomplish.

This point in your entrepreneurial journey is a pivotal moment: the proverbial fork in the road. The direction you choose is going to have a lasting impact on your business. You recognize the need for additional resources to manage the business, but the thought of increasing your overhead by taking on an employee is scary.

However, if you don't take on more resources, you'll stagnate at your current level of business.

So how do you know when it's the right time to hire your first employee? When the business is ready. When *you* are ready. And when adding employees is in strategic alignment with your vision for the business.

Finding the Help You Need

You begin by going right back to your business plan and reviewing your vision. If your goal is to build a sustainable business enterprise, then it's going to take more than one set of hands to get there. If it's not, then it may be time to scale back a little so you can manage your business effectively and professionally by yourself. Remember the discussion in Chapter 1 about the difference between creating a job and creating a business.

Step One: Identify Your Needs

Ready to take on the challenge of building a truly sustainable enterprise? Then examine what's happening in your business right now. Are things starting to slip through the cracks? Are you missing deadlines? Are you reaching the point of being burned out? Any of these situations can be indicators that it's time to bring someone on board to assist you—especially if you see your currently burgeoning business levels continuing to increase, rather than being a short-term or seasonal situation.

My strategy for adding employees is what I call MYTOP, or *multiply yourself through other people*. Your first employee should be someone who complements your skill set so that you can focus your time and energy on the things you do well and that add the most value to your business. So before you hire anyone, identify and analyze your own strengths and weaknesses.

Here is a worksheet to help you assess your skills. It lists the characteristics needed to grow a successful business. Rate yourself in each of the following areas.

Business Function	EXCELLENT	SATISFACTORY	POOR
Marketing Communications			
Sales (making calls and presentations)			
Business Development (strategic alliances)			
Sales & Development Management (building a team and establishing goals)			
Account Management			
Operations (business processes)			
Managing Employees (HR functions)			
Financial Management (general accounting)			
Business and Strategic Planning			
Financial Analysis (making projections/ budgets)			
Technology (internal tech support)			
Technology Development (identifying technology applications for business growth)			
Website/Database Management			
Product Development			
Pricing			
Public Relations/Public Outreach/ Spokesperson			
Clerical/Administrative			
Other:			

You might ask someone with whom you have worked closely in the past to fill out this worksheet about you to get another's perspective on your strengths and weaknesses. Sometimes we don't see things in ourselves that others can see. It certainly doesn't hurt to have additional input.

After reviewing the completed worksheet, make your first hire someone who has abilities in the areas where you are the weakest. Most often, your weaknesses will correlate with the things you don't like doing, so why not bring in someone who is good at those things and enjoys doing them, too?

Step Two: Determine and Convey Exactly What You Want

After you've settled on the skills that would be most helpful to you, write a job description for a position that encompasses those skills. Yes, I realize this is challenging because, since the job never existed, you're not yet sure what the job is going to entail. It doesn't matter. You still need to map out the responsibilities of the position and document it before you start your search.

To identify the right candidate, it's important to establish your expectations. This is also important for your new employee. Without articulating your specific expectations, the chances of your new hire failing are great. And that will be frustrating and unpleasant for both of you.

During a question-and-answer session at one of my seminars on building a successful business enterprise, an attendee wanted to know why she couldn't seem to find a good administrative assistant. She told me how several people she'd hired for the position hadn't worked out, and she was ready to give up. She concluded that there wasn't anyone out there to fit the job. Then I asked the obvious question: "Do you have a job description that lays out expectations?"

The woman responded with a vague "sure," mumbled, and gave rambling explanations. So I asked again . . . and again. Finally, she admitted that she hadn't actually written anything down. Voilà! Problem identified. If you don't know *specifically* what you expect the new hire to do for your business, then don't be surprised when it doesn't work out. Take the time to draft a comprehensive job description before you begin your employee search.

Step Three: Determine the Salary Range

Before you conduct an employee search, determine the salary range for the position. Committing to a salary amount is scary. But you need to recognize that, in order to hire the type and caliber of individual who can help you grow your business, you may have to take a salary cut yourself. In fact, many entrepreneurs find they have to miss a paycheck here and there in order to make sure their employees are paid. Are you ready to make that sacrifice? It's another type of financial investment in your business. However, if you choose employees wisely, the rewards will come because two people can accomplish far more than can one.

Step Four: Hire Smart, Not Fast

Always strive to hire people who are smarter than you are. Entrepreneurs tend to have large egos—we like to think we know it all. But the smartest people are the ones who are willing to admit they don't know everything. And they are the most successful because they hire people who fill their knowledge gaps. Also, make sure that whoever you hire is at the top of his or her game—someone with a proven track record of success.

However, avoid hiring the big-company star. To grow your small business, you'll need someone who knows how to get things done without a big budget and a big staff. The big-company star may look good on paper, but often they don't know how to get great results with limited resources. They are super at developing big-picture strategies, delegating responsibility, and outsourcing tasks, but they don't know how to dig the hole themselves. Look for someone who has worked in an entrepreneurial environment.

Family and Friends—Oh, No!

"I can't get everything done. I need someone NOW!"

Behold the rant of the frantic small-business owners who haven't planned to hire smart. Now they have their backs against a wall and they rush out to hire the first warm body available: Usually this means a friend or a family member. But before you decide to hire a friend or a family member, consider whether the person has the skills, experience, and core competencies you need to grow your business.

I'd say that 90 percent of the time, hiring family or friends ends in disaster. When things go awry, long-term friendships are destroyed and family gatherings become extremely uncomfortable. My two uncles didn't speak to each other for about five years thanks to a bad business deal. Every holiday, my mom struggled with seating arrangements and made every possible accommodation to avoid an ugly scene between them. I'm sure that's not something you want, so think before you leap into the arms of family or friends.

As a cash-strapped small-business start-up, what do you do if a friend or family member is willing to work for free or for a below-market-value salary? Remember: You get what you pay for. Typically, your friends and family mean well, they want you to succeed, and they think they are doing you a favor. But the operative word here is *favor*. When someone thinks he or she is helping you out and doing you a favor, then it's not a "real" job and you aren't really the "boss." Chances are, the individual won't take you or the job seriously, and could easily leave you high and dry when you need the person the most.

But let's say that, after careful consideration, you decide the family member or friend does make sense for your business. In that case, make the employment a professional business relationship, with the roles, responsibilities, and expectations clearly defined and agreed upon. I recommend putting everything in writing, because memories are very short.

When you have a friend or family member on the payroll, personal baggage is a critical consideration. Family conflicts should be dealt with outside the office, so customers or other employees aren't caught in the middle. And, if and when you add more staff, make sure you don't show favoritism, because doing so will damage company morale in a hurry. When you make a decision concerning an employee who is a friend or family member, stop and ask yourself whether you'd make the same decision if you didn't have the personal connection. It's logic, not emotion, that must control your thought process, and with friends and family that can be difficult.

Ask yourself whether the friend or family member has the ability and desire to grow and evolve as your company expands. What will you do if your business grows and the person is no longer a good fit? Will you be comfortable letting the person go? Will the person recognize the time to exit gracefully? Think about that before you agree to hire.

Finally, consider the possibility of having to let the friend or family member go. According to Chris Kelleher, of The Law Firm for Businesses PC, a legal organization that caters to small-business people, "this type of termination isn't 'just business.' It's often very personal and can easily harm and even destroy friendships and family relationships." He adds, "If there is no other choice than to terminate the employment relationship, then the business owner must wear two hats: one as an employer and the other as a family member or friend. Regardless of how well this type of termination is handled from both perspectives, the business owner must realize that the personal or family relationship may not survive."

As with all entrepreneurial business decisions, the final choice is yours, but I encourage you to think long and hard before adding that friend or family member to your team. Employees come and go, but we hope and trust our friends and families are here to stay.

The Employee Turned Competitor

About once a week I appear on a television program called *Good Money*. The program airs on *ABC News Now*, and my segment is branded "Minding Your Business with Susan Solovic." During the second part of my segment, viewers call in to the program with questions related to small-business operations.

On one program's call-in segment, Eric, who had successfully grown his marketing business over several years, explained that he had reached the pivotal moment when he felt he needed an employee to help him manage his current workload so he'd have more time to add new clients. Eric's hesitation about adding staff wasn't concern for financial risk; it was the prospect of training someone on the unique strategies he used for his clients, then watching that employee take the knowledge and perhaps start his own firm or go to work for a competitor.

My response was, yes, that can happen, and it is a risk every business owner takes. Whether it is intellectual property, a customer list, or even something as simple as excellent hands-on training, employees may leave after training and take valuable information with them. (For example, my father groomed a young man in the funeral business, taking him in as an apprentice and teaching him the business for over 20 years. Then, we learned from a family friend that the man was in the process of building a new funeral home and at night was copying my family's business files. My parents and I confronted him, and he confirmed what we'd been told. We asked him to leave immediately. He cried and said he was sorry, but the damage was done. Fortunately, as long as my parents continued to own and operate their own business, it continued to prosper, and the community supported them, while the former employee, buried in debt, struggled to build his business.)

There are two important things you need to accept when it comes to risking competition from an employee:

1. You can't build a successful, sustainable business without a team. Remember MYTOP: *multiply yourself through other people*.

2. There are plenty of unethical people in this world, and someday one of them may end up working for you. It is part of the risk of building a business.

There are, however, a few things you can do to protect your business as you build your staff:

• Make your company a place where people want to work. Create an environment that's empowering and fun. Give your staff the opportunity to profit as the business profits. When you help people to feel part of the success, there is less incentive for them to leave and they are more likely to remain loyal. (Think back to the purpose, promise, and principles of your business. They will help you establish a good corporate culture and work environment.)

• Ask employees to sign a noncompcte/nondisclosure agreement as a condition of employment. Noncompcte documents must be reasonable in time and scope, and you cannot bar an individual from making a living except to the extent that it is necessary to protect your business. The extent to which noncompete documents are allowable varies by jurisdiction, so it is a good idea to consult with your business attorney.

Some people believe noncompete agreements don't provide much value, but in my opinion they minimize the risk of an employee jumping ship and working for a competitor or starting his or her own business. At least when employees sign these documents, they are aware that there may be serious consequences for actions that could cost you business. If my father had asked his employee to sign a noncompete document, most likely the employee would not have been able to launch a competing business in the same area. An important lesson learned.

Always consult with your legal adviser regarding noncompete/nondisclosure documents.

Evaluate Your Options

Instead of hiring someone full-time, you may have other options for getting help, such as temporary staffing, independent contractors, freelancers, or virtual assistants. Because these workers are not actual employees of your business, you pay only for what you use. This option can help you better manage your cash flow, because you avoid overhead costs involved with employees, such as payroll taxes, unemployment insurance, worker's compensation, and Social Security taxes. Additionally, you may also avoid fringe benefits such as healthcare coverage, retirement options, and vacation and sick days.

Temporary staffing agencies provide the added benefit of helping you find the right employees. They advertise, screen, interview, test, and check references and backgrounds. (In fact, one staffing agency I worked with helped me more clearly define the job description for a position, which helped me to better identify the right candidate for the job.) Once the temporary employee is on board, the agency also takes care of all the payroll and taxes, so you don't have to worry about that, either.

Among the alternatives for obtaining help may be outsourcing the work (i.e., to an independent contractor, a virtual assistant, or a freelancer). These workers may be contracted on a project basis or an ongoing basis, but in either case you still pay only for the work they actually do for you. Technically, they are operating their own businesses, and can have other clients at the same time. Plus, because they operate their own businesses, they pay their own taxes and expenses, which saves you money.

Small businesses like using independent contractors because it saves them money. However, don't be penny-wise and dollar-foolish. The IRS looks very closely at the way employees classify workers. Misclassification of a worker as an independent contractor rather than an employee can be a costly mistake, making you potentially liable for back taxes and penalties—and possibly even criminal charges. And in some cases, misclassified workers have sued their employers for lost benefits during the time they should have been considered employees.

To aid employers in determining the correct status of a worker, the IRS has established a list of guidelines to consider. You can find them on the IRS website (www.irs.gov) but I have highlighted some of the key factors below.

- *Working relationship.* Does the worker have other clients for whom he or she works or does the individual work exclusively for you? An independent contractor is in business for him- or herself, so there should be other clients, or the person should at least be available to acquire other business opportunities.

- *Working hours.* Employees typically have their work hours scheduled; whereas an independent contractor can establish his or her own work hours as long as the contractor meets the deadline established by the client.

• *Work location.* Generally, an independent contractor provides his or her own work location, materials, and equipment. Although the worker may need to perform some of the work at your facility, his or her primary office is the one he or she provides.

• *Execution.* Employees are assigned projects and given direction on how to perform the work. They are also provided with any equipment they may need. An independent contractor, on the other hand, will determine how to complete the work and will utilize his or her own equipment and materials.

• *Expenses.* Employees typically submit their work-related expenses to their employers for reimbursement. An independent contractor, however, generally absorbs expenses as part of the cost of doing business.

• *Taxes.* An independent contractor pays his or her own taxes by filing quarterly estimated tax returns. Your company does not withhold taxes.

• *Business indicators.* An independent contractor should have a variety of indicators that demonstrate self-employment. Business cards, marketing materials, and/or a website are all indications that the individual is truly independent. Another indicator is whether or not the worker has established a legal entity for his or her company, such as a corporation or limited liability company.

If after reviewing the IRS guidelines you are still confused about the status of a worker, the IRS can make the determination for you if you file a form SS-8, which is also available on the IRS website (www.irs.gov).

There are other drawbacks to hiring independent contractors. Because they are in business for themselves, they may not always be available when you need them. Plus, keep in mind that if an independent contractor becomes an integral part of your business operations, and then you lose the contractor for whatever reason, you may be left in the lurch. You'll have to find someone else and familiarize the new person with your business needs.

The Hiring Process

Once you know the type of individual you want to add to your team, have written the job description, and have decided on a salary range, you begin the search. Where do you go to find the people to help you realize your business vision?

The best place to start is within your own business network. Reach out to others whom you respect and let them know you are searching for a qualified candidate. Many business owners and managers are finding themselves in the difficult position of laying off good employees, and they would welcome the opportunity to refer those people whenever possible. (However, keep in mind the importance of identifying a candidate who has entrepreneurial experience or mindset.) Additionally, almost all businesspeople have friends and former colleagues who are in the process of a job search. For me, networking has always proven to be the best way to find high-quality individuals.

Social media sites are increasingly popular recruiting tools for small buinesses, particularly LinkedIn. I get at least six inquiries from companies each month with specific job postings; they have used their LinkedIn memberships to identify qualified job candidates. Through that website, they notify their contacts and ask for help in finding someone to meet their business needs. While I have never done this myself, I know people who have had tremendous success utilizing this resource.

Job-posting websites are another way to launch an employee search. Most sites are not very expensive and are easy to use. If you post your job opening in the newspaper, you're stuck with whatever gets printed. Online sites, however, give you flexibility to make changes in your posting if you see you aren't getting the type of responses you need.

Staffing agencies, although more expensive, can be well worth the money. Typically, you pay a staffing agency a percentage of the employee's first-year annual salary. However, just as with a temporary staffing agency, they will help you refine the job description, establish a fair-market salary range, prescreen all candidates, conduct testing, and undertake the necessary background and reference checks. If you've never had any experience hiring employees, a staffing agency could be a smart way to go.

Hire the Best Candidate, Not the Best Job Seeker

In the quest to find the most talented employees, many business owners wind up with the most talented job seekers instead. Choosing the wrong applicant can be a costly mistake. While there is no method of hiring that guarantees you'll get it right every time, there are things you can do to minimize mistakes:

• *Brush up on your interviewing skills.* An interview requires a considerable amount of preparation. Don't "wing it," and don't ask standard textbook questions. Think about what it is you want to accomplish during the interview. What types of information would be helpful to you in evaluating a candidate's ability to do the job?

• *Use an evaluation sheet.* If you're going to be interviewing multiple candidates, record your impressions on an evaluation sheet. This will help you measure each candidate by the same criteria, and it will also help you keep the individuals straight in your mind. I don't know about you, but after a few interviews, particularly if they are on the same day, I can get confused about who said what.

• *Look beyond the résumé.* Try not to go through a reiteration of the candidate's résumé. You already have that on hand and can verify any of the information provided. What you need to find out is what makes the job applicant tick, and whether or not she or he is going to be the right fit for your business.

• *Ask open-ended questions.* Ask questions that solicit fuller responses. Take notes. Avoid the temptation to do all the talking. You want to learn about the individual. Ask what he or she liked most and/or least about the previous working environment. Find out about the person's accomplishments. Present a typical business situation the candidate would encounter with your firm and ask how he or she would handle it.

• *Assess character.* One of the keys to finding the right employee is to identify who is a good fit for your company culture. The most talented individual in the world will cause serious problems for your business if he or she isn't the right fit, character-wise. Skills can be taught, but you can't change someone's personality and character.

I didn't listen to my own advice once when it came to hiring a new employee. Not only did I pay the price, but so did my team. My choice had been between two job applicants; one had slightly more digital media experience than the other, but the one with less experience seemed a better personality fit. What did I do? I hired the one with more experience.

He was a bad fit from the very first day. In the end, he slammed the door to our executive producer's office and marched back to his office. I followed closely on his heels and dismissed him on the spot. Such behavior was not something I tolerated. Fortunately, less than a month had elapsed and the other candidate was still available. He joined the team and he was fabulous.

The Situational Interview

Situational interviews can help you to move beyond the résumé and get a better sense of the candidate's true abilities. If left to frame their own responses to your questions, people can spin their qualifications in a way that doesn't accurately portray how they would really perform on the job. A situational interview, however, is like a work-related test. Research shows that situational interviews are about 50 percent more effective than traditional interviews and more predictive of future success on the job. However, since they do involve more work for the candidate, don't use them unless you are serious about him or her.

What's a situational interview? It's best understood with an example. Say a public relations firm is looking for a new hire. They might ask the potential employee to role-play a client meeting or write a press release. Or they might create a case study of a typical situation the employee might encounter on the job and ask what steps he or she would take to manage it.

Make sure the framework you use for the situational interview closely matches the exact job requirements. To the best of your ability, establish objective judging criteria in advance of the interview. If you have other staff members who'll be working with the new employee, ask them to meet the candidate and provide input for evaluation, too.

The Interview Boundaries

Familiarize yourself with what are deemed inappropriate and/or illegal interview questions. Questions relating to marital status, age, religious or political affiliation, and so on, are off limits. A potential employer cannot discuss these matters, even indirectly. The Equal Employment Opportunity Commission offers interview guidelines (www.eeoc.gov). If you are still unsure of the boundaries, and know someone who is a human resources professional, he or she would be a good reference, too. Don't think that because you are a small company, you are exempt from these federal and state antidiscrimination laws.

References and Background

Never rely on your instincts alone when judging potential employees. "Trust but verify" is my motto. Negligent hiring can lead to a lawsuit if your employee hurts someone while on the job. Failure to check backgrounds has resulted in embezzlements, stolen equipment, stolen customer identification, and, in the worst case—violence.

Partnership: Thumbs Up or Thumbs Down?

Initially, or as your business takes off, you may consider partnership as a way to build your business. There are pros and cons:

- "Most lawyers say don't do it." —Jeremy Nulik, editor, *St. Louis Small Business Monthly*.

- "Good ones are hard to find. I have had an excellent business partner for more than four years and I am grateful for our collective efforts and talents. My situation is one in a million though." —Michelle Bain, entrepreneur and creator of Thumbs Up Johnnie.

- "Nope. Hire people. Too much trouble disconnecting, and you marry their issues as well." —Karen Krymski, of the think tank Women Power UP!

- "Thumbs down, down, down. If you do opt for a partner, make sure one of you has the majority share even if it's only one percent more; otherwise you'll constantly be in a stalemate." —Iris Salsman, owner of Salsman PR, a public relations firm.

For many years, I was totally against the idea of bringing partners into a small business. There are myriad examples of businesses that have folded because of failed partnerships. In fact, I would venture a guess that a failed partnership is among the top reasons for business failure.

A business partnership is a lot like a romantic one. When you're just getting started with the partnership, everything appears to be wonderful—like the first blush of romance. You get caught up in the excitement, and you can't imagine anything going wrong. But as the relationship progresses, problems and disagreements arise. Some issues are easily dealt with, but others may become insurmountable. So, while I point out the pros and cons of this business situation, it is up to you to decide what will work best for your business venture.

Thumbs Up

Partnerships created for the right reasons can help a business grow more rapidly. If you bring a partner into your business, the person should add value and in some way complement what you offer the business. With ItsYourBiz.com, I've had two partners, each of whom had different skill sets from my own. One was an expert in the technology field (he is deceased) and the other had spent the majority of his career building and managing sales organizations. By combining our expertise we were able to accomplish more in a shorter period of time.

When Peggy Traub, the founder of Adesso lighting, a specialty lighting manufacturer, decided to start her business, she sought out as a partner the best person she knew in the industry in terms of sales and product development. She shared with me that when she first envisioned her company she realized that although she had great retail experience, she would need a partner who knew the manufacturing and sales side of the business—an area where she had limited experience. As a result, she identified someone she knew to be an expert, and proposed her concept. When she approached him, he recognized the opportunity and together they were able to build a highly successful company.

That's how I chose my business partners, too. Early on I analyzed what it would take to build then SBTV.com into what I envisioned, and I realized I needed both technological expertise and someone who had extensive sales experience. Could I have *hired* people with those skills? Certainly. But just as with many small-business start-ups, I didn't have the funds to hire the type of skilled individuals I needed to build the business. Instead, finding partners who had these skills and shared my vision made the business development more achievable.

Partnerships bring more than just diversity in skill sets. They also provide diversity in perspective, which can be healthy for a new company. By looking at business challenges from different points of view, you often discover unique solutions. Of course, that also means you will have disagreements at times; but as long as you deal with them in a productive way, the differing perspectives can be beneficial.

The right partner may be someone who has important connections. Like it or not, as the saying goes, business is often more about who you know than what you know. So if you need someone who can open doors for you, a well-connected partner could be a smart move.

Finally, a partner may be a financing source. As you know by now, finding capital to start and grow your business is difficult. Therefore, partners who can invest money in the business can be beneficial. However, before you take any investment money from anyone, make sure you have the appropriate legal documents in place. For that, you should consult with an attorney.

Thumbs Down

The primary problem with partnerships is conflict. And it's safe to say there is conflict in 99 percent of all business partnerships. Conflict arises over the direction of the company; conflict occurs when one partner feels as though he or she is doing all the work; conflict is paramount when core values clash. Even if you choose partners based on business needs, you can't ignore the importance of shared values and vision. Without the right tools to manage conflict, the business will suffer significantly. Just as with a bad marriage, when the problems start, emotions run high and often emotion supersedes good judgment.

Let me share with you my costly lesson in relation to partnerships. (I refer to this as my expensive MBA.) When I had a boutique advertising and public relations firm, I landed a major client that became about 90 percent of my business. The client company was owned 50/50 by a husband and wife. The wife caught the husband with another woman—and it got ugly. She said yes to something, and he said no. My invoices stopped getting paid. The company was in chaos. One day, their employees showed up to work and there was a sign on the door informing them that the company was out of business. The two owners had left town, separately, and that was the end of the story. The company's subsequent bankruptcy nearly put me in bankruptcy, too.

It's Your Choice

So, if you think a partnership might be the right decision for your business, remember these things:

• You need a partnership agreement that clearly defines how decisions will be made and what happens if the parties can't agree. The agreement should also describe how the partnership can be broken up. In other words, it is like a prenuptial agreement: How are we going to divide things up when we can't get along anymore?

• If it's possible, you should maintain the controlling interest in your business. If that's not possible, then include language in your partnership agreement that requires a supermajority vote on major issues. Otherwise, you could find yourself locked out of your own company.

• Be careful about going into a business partnership with a friend or a family member. As I noted earlier, employing friends and family is a sticky issue. Partnerships are even more involved, and a failed partnership can be even more damaging.

Getting Great Advice

Starting and growing a business is a complex process, and by now I hope you've realized it is impossible for you to know everything. The more information, talent, and resources you can access, the greater your chances of success. Advisory boards, mentors, and business coaches can help.

Advisory Boards

No matter how small or large your firm is, you can benefit from building an advisory board. Think about the last time you met with other businesspeople and had an open discussion about your business challenges. Talking through various issues with others can often help you identify strategies you may not have seen before. An advisory board formalizes this process.

Having an advisory board is also a cost-effective way for your small business to gain critical expertise so you can adjust your course as necessary. Board members may also be able to open doors for you by utilizing their networks. Because advisory boards are not formally part of your company, they don't run the risk of fiduciary or legal liability. The advice they share with you is nonbinding. Entrepreneurs are often eternal optimists, and while this is not necessarily a bad thing, it can have its disadvantages. Sometimes we miss the red flags because of our "can-do" attitude. A strong advisory board can help you avoid potential obstacles.

Determine how many people you want to serve on your board. Too many people often results in lower productivity. Therefore, consider having no more than a handful of people, and choose them wisely. In fact, selecting the right individuals for your board is critical. Again, consider complementing your own personal skills and strengths. Make a list of the areas where you need the most help, and use this list to identify advisory board members who can complement your attributes.

Remember to look for people who are strong enough to take unpopular stances and give you honest feedback. A "yes" person isn't right for this group. It's also critical that your board members understand the dynamics of a small business and the challenges of your industry. And you should consider whether you are truly willing to listen to advice that runs counter to your ideas. Many business founders are so confident in their own ideas that they become defensive and miss essential information.

To get the most benefit from your advisory board meetings, always be prepared for them. Choose a location for the meeting that is free of distractions. It's a good idea to distribute essential information in advance of the meeting so your board members have time to review it. After your meetings, keep the lines of communication with your board members open. The fact that they've agreed to serve on your board means that they care about your success. Keep them updated on your company's progress. And remember: Ideas without action aren't worth much. It's up to you to take action.

By the way, I sit on a number of advisory boards for small businesses and I am always honored to be asked, so don't be hesitant to invite people. Honestly, I get a lot out of the meetings and enjoy learning about a variety of businesses.

Mentors

One of the best ways to enhance your opportunity for success is to find a business mentor. There are lots of resources providing basic business information on starting and growing a business, but a business mentor goes far beyond that. Mentors provide valuable insight that you can't find anywhere else.

"Mentoring" is a term historically used to describe a teacher-student relationship. In the business world, though, mentoring occurs when a more experienced professional (the mentor) gives significant career assistance to a less-experienced professional (the protégé). Mentoring relationships are helpful during every stage of business development, from start-up to exit. A mentor's knowledge, experience, tenacity, and skills offer the growing entrepreneur guidance, advice, and training. Some of the most successful business owners openly attribute much of their success to a mentor or mentors.

So how do you go about finding a mentor? Through myriad small-business organizations and associations, you'll find structured small-business programs that provide mentors. While these are good, helpful programs, I personally think the best mentor relationships are the ones you create on your own. Now you are thinking, how do I find a mentor on my own?

Finding a mentor takes time and patience. After all, you want someone with the right expertise and experience. Start your hunt close to home. Think about your family, friends, and even close business colleagues. Even if they don't have the experience you need, they may know someone who does. Be prepared to explain what kind of help you need or the type of person you are looking for. Reach out to your personal network, too. Once again, be specific about your particular needs. Most businesspeople recognize the value of finding mentors and are happy to help you or make suggestions.

Could your mentor be an absolute stranger? Absolutely. Think about successful businesspeople whom you admire. And they don't have to be in your geographic area. You can enjoy a successful mentoring relationship via long distance. I'm frequently approached by people who ask me to be their mentor. Personally, I am flattered, and I think most people are.

The first thing a potential mentor will ask is, "What are your expectations?" So you'll need to know how to answer that question. Define the parameters of what you'd like and be reasonable about time expectations. Keep in mind that if you ask a highly successful business owner to be your mentor, you can't expect her or him to commit endless hours to you.

Also, mentors are not "answer men"—they're not there to tell you what to do. Don't expect them to make you successful. You're responsible for your own success. They are just there to serve as guides.

Business Coaches

Coaching small businesses is a hot business in itself. Over the past decade or so, coaches have popped up like mushrooms after the rain. A top-quality business coach can be a tremendous asset to your business. Coaching can help you bridge the gap between where you are today and where you want to be tomorrow. A good coach can help you sort things out—what is not working and what you would like to see happen. In many respects, what you get from a business coach is the ability to develop a deeper understanding of where your magic lies.

But all coaches are not created equal. Some specialize in life coaching; others are focused on business coaching. To ensure that you get quality assistance, it is important to choose wisely. Don't be shy about asking about their background and training. For example, look for a coach who has experience working with entrepreneurs and who has been in the business for a while. Coaching is a competitive business, so if someone has survived successfully for a number of years, they probably have something going for them.

Ask other business professionals for referrals. And before you decide to work with a particular coach, ask for references. Many coaches are picky about the clients with whom they work, which is smart. That's a good sign, because by limiting the number of clients, they will have more time to focus on you. It also demonstrates that they understand the importance of establishing the right relationship dynamics. Most especially, it's important to find a coach with whom you feel comfortable. You need to feel secure enough to reveal significant details about your business and your own personal feelings.

But selecting a coach is only one side of the coin. The other side is you. Most business owners turn to coaches when they have had some success in their business but they know they need to do more to get to the next level. The critical point: You have to be ready to be helped. You have to have the right mindset to benefit from what a coach can offer.

Are you ready to hear what you might not want to hear? It is a coach's job to take an objective look at what is happening in your business and ask tough questions. The coach is also going to provide insight into how you are personally managing your business. You may not be prepared to deal with this feedback, and as a result you may throw up your defenses. If that's the case, you might as well stop right there, because you're not ready to be coached.

Coaches charge fees for their services, so remember that you get what you pay for. Quality coaches aren't going to be cheap, but good coaches do have the skills to spur you on to greater success.

CHAPTER 8

---

protecting your business, your ideas, and yourself

WHEN YOU START a business, hiring pricey professionals probably won't be high on your list of ways to spend money. You may think to yourself that lawyers and CPAs mean big bucks, and you don't have money to burn. But the case for hiring a professional accountant is fairly easy to make: You'll need someone to help you set up your books professionally and to make sure you don't get in trouble with the Internal Revenue Service (IRS). (More about tax issues later in the chapter.)

The case for hiring an attorney isn't as obvious, so a lot of small businesses just start off without any professional legal advice. Perhaps they just aren't knowledgeable about the legal complexities involved with starting a business. Some new business owners believe that unless they're involved in a risky business, there's no need to worry about establishing a legal structure for their business. Other owners realize there are legal issues to adddress, but they don't want to spend the money right away, and they think they can get by for a while without doing so.

To save money, many new entrepreneurs choose to use the do-it-yourself legal options available today. You can get forms from your state's secretary of state's office or find them on legal information websites. Many of these options are satisfactory, but they should not *replace* professional legal advice. I recommend that you then invest in having all your legal documents reviewed by an attorney before you finalize everything.

I know that with a plethora of information at your fingertips, it is easy to imagine that you can handle all the legal work on your own. But keep in mind that not everything is black-and-white. The language used on forms seems straightforward, but it's never as simple as it appears. One could easily assume the lawyers who created the forms deliberately made them confusing for job security reasons. But as an attorney, I can assure you that's not true. There are nuances involved with making legal decisions about your company, and unless you have the legal training, you couldn't possibly understand them. If you wait until you're dealing with a legal problem to hire an attorney, you'll generally find it's too late. And talk about racking up legal fees—just watch the billable hours churn away as prior work is cleared up. The fees you'll pay for legal services in advance of a problem are insignificant compared to what you'll pay an attorney to get you out of trouble. Plus, dealing with legal problems creates an emotional and productivity drain on you and your business. So be proactive. Make an attorney and an accountant important parts of your start-up team. It will be money well spent.

A Perfect Case in Point

In Chapter 6, we talked about what's in a name. If you decided to do business under a name other than your own, or the legal name of your corporation, then the law requires you to file what's known as a "fictitious name registration." You've probably heard it referred to as a DBA, or "doing business as. . . ." For example, if I decided to launch a catering business as a sole proprietor and call it Susan Solovic's Meals to Go, I wouldn't have to file a fictitious name registration because the business has my name in it. However, if I called my catering business Mainly Meals, then I'd need to file the fictitious name registration. Why is this? Primarily because if someone needs to sue Mainly Meals, the public needs to know who is behind that business. The fictitious name registration shows I am the owner of that name. The same would be true if I had incorporated as Solovic Enterprises Catering, Inc., and then wanted to do business as Mainly Meals. Solovic Enterprises Catering, Inc., would need to be noted in public records as the owner of the name Mainly Meals.

During the brief period I practiced law, five male friends decided to incorporate their business on their own. When you incorporate, you can select a name for your company as long as no other business has already registered that name. So my friends named their company ABC, Inc.

After they incorporated, they decided they didn't like the name they had chosen for their business and they wanted to operate under a different name. So they filed a fictitious name registration for Five Guys Biz. About one year later, I received a frantic call from one of the quintet. They'd all been sued personally by a creditor of their business. "They can't sue us personally," my friend exclaimed. "We're incorporated!"

So I called the attorney who filed the suit against them and asked why he sued them individually instead of suing the corporation. "Have you seen their fictitious name registration?" he asked. When I admitted I hadn't, he smugly agreed to fax it to me. (We were still using faxes then.)

As soon as I read the document, I knew my friends were in trouble. As I noted, corporations can transact business under a name that's different from their official one by filing a fictitious name registration that states that this company is now operating with this name. However, that's not what my friends' paperwork indicated. It said the five of them were doing business individually under the new name. That's why the attorney was able to bring suit against them personally instead of their corporation. Ultimately we settled the case, but the expense put them out of business.

How to Hire an Attorney

Finding the right professional advisers is important. Don't rely on your family attorney or your friend's buddy unless you are confident he or she has the experience you need. You'll need an attorney who specializes in business law for small to midsize businesses. Other business owners are often the best source of referral. Find out whom they trust and what they like about their attorneys. Generally speaking, lawyers are not warm and fuzzy people. (I can say that, since I am one.) So if someone talks about his or her attorney in glowing terms, that's a good indication that the individual is someone you can count on for your business needs.

You'll also need an attorney who speaks in plain English. Unless you've gone through law school or have worked in areas related to business law, you can't be expected to understand all the legal jargon. A good attorney will patiently explain things in terms that you, a business owner, can easily comprehend. No attorney should ever talk down to you or make you feel foolish for not being familiar with the legal mumbo jumbo. You should feel comfortable asking as many questions as you'd like. Remember—the only dumb questions are the ones you *don't* ask. After all, it's your business, and any decisions you make resulting from legal advice may affect your success. In fact, if you don't feel comfortable with the advice you've received, there's nothing wrong with getting a second opinion, just as you would if you had a medical problem.

Which is better—a lawyer in a small firm or one in a large firm? That depends. Theoretically, a sole practitioner or a lawyer in a small firm will have lower fees than a big-firm attorney. However, don't rule out a large firm if your concern is just the cost. Large firms have associates and paralegals who often do much of the work at lower hourly rates. And the benefit of working with a large law firm is that it has more clout. In other words, if you ever have a legal problem, a letter from a prestigious firm is going to be more intimidating than one from a local attorney who works out of his or her home.

Since lawyers are in business to make money, that means they need clients. So don't be afraid to negotiate fees or request a fixed price for a particular project. A fixed fee allows you to budget for the expense so you can better manage your cash flow.

Finally, always check an attorney's references and see whether there are any complaints filed against him or her with the Bar Association in your state and the American Bar Association.

Protecting Yourself from Personal Liability

There are four basic organizational structures that apply to small-business operations: sole proprietorship, partnership, coporation, and limited liability company (LLC). I'm frequently asked: "Do I need a formal organization structure for my business to make it legal?" First, as long as you're not running a business that's against the law, then your business is automatically legal. (I actually heard a college business school dean refer to small businesses as being legal and illegal. I couldn't believe it.) The real question is whether or not you want to establish a legal structure for your business. The primary reason you should strongly consider it is to protect yourself from personal liability.

Some people assume that they don't need to establish a legal structure for their business because they believe, or have been advised, that there is very little risk associated with operating their business. Cautiously, I would say that's true for some small-business ventures, such as a hobby business or a part-time business for which you have no plans of expanding to a full-time enterprise. Still, even if you're in a small operation, you are not automatically safe. These days anyone can—and does—sue anyone for anything. Believe me, there is an attorney out there who will take the case, and suddenly you'll find yourself in court even if there's little or no justification.

If you don't have a legal structure for your business, and you happen to lose the suit, then the judgment will be against you personally. As a result, your personal financial well-being could be significantly harmed and the judgment could damage your reputation and future business opportunities. However, when you establish a formal legal structure for your business, creditors of the business normally can't go after your personal assets to pay your business debts and/or claims arising from lawsuits. (There are exceptions so, again, consult with a legal professional.)

The structure you choose for your business will have long-term implications, so it's important to choose wisely. Consider the big-picture vision you have for your company (see Chapter 1). Some types of legal structures limit your ability to raise capital, so if you foresee that, down the road, you might need investment capital to build the business, then your entity choice is critical. It's also important to carefully review the tax consequences of the various legal structures. An accountant or attorney can explain the tax implications to you or you can do your own research on the Internet. However, be careful that, if you resort to the Internet, you make sure you obtain your information from a trustworthy site, such as the IRS or Small Business Administration (SBA), or a specialized legal resource site such as LegalZoom.com, BizFilings.com, Company Corporation.com, or NoloPress.com.

What Type of Legal Structure Do I Need?

Although there are a number of organizational structures that could apply to a small business, the four types I mentioned previously are the most common. What follows is an overview of each.

Sole Proprietorship

The easiest and quickest way to start a business is as a sole proprietorship. Why? Because all you really need to do is to start. In fact, you may already have a sole proprietorship and not even know it. If you do any freelance work, sell merchandise on Interent sites such as eBay or Craigslist, market crafts on the weekend at a flea market, or pick up odd jobs now and then without an established business structure, then by default you are a sole proprietorship.

Even though a sole proprietorship is simple to set up, that doesn't mean you can forgo good business-management practices. You will still need to set up and maintain a professional bookkeeping system to keep track of business income and expenses, separate from personal ones.

For tax purposes, a sole proprietorship is what is known as a "pass-through entity." Legally, it isn't separate from you as an individual, so at tax time you report all business income or losses on an IRS Schedule C form, which is filed with your personal income tax.

Keep in mind, however, that even though establishing a sole proprietorship doesn't require any special legal filings, there may be other legal issues to consider, such as business licenses and permits. Make sure you check with your local municipality and a professional adviser such as your CPA or attorney. The secretary of state's office in your state may have a checklist you can use to ensure you follow the proper procedures.

The key points of a sole proprietorship are:

- No filings required with the state

- Owned and operated by a single individual

- No protection from personal liability

- Limited ability to raise funds

Partnership

Partnerships are much like sole proprietorships, but they are for two or more individuals To create a partnership, all you have to do is decide to go into business with someone else. No legal filings are required.

However, there are perils to partnerships that obviously don't apply when you're working in a sole proprietorship. For example, the word "partner" is used liberally in business conversation without much regard for the implications of its use. If you hold someone out to the public as your partner, and it is reasonable for the public to rely on that representation, then you could be legally bound for any and all actions of that individual regardless of the true nature of your relationship. So if you are in a partnership—real or perceived—the actions of one partner bind the other partners and each can individually and separately be held responsible for the whole. As an example, simply stated: If your partner commits fraud and skips the country, you'll be left holding the bag. So be careful about how you use the term. And remember, as with a sole proprietorship, a partnership provides no protection from personal liability.

If you decide a partnership is right for you, then make sure you have a partnership agreement in place. I have seen many "friends" decide to go into business as partners. Excited about their new business venture, and secure in their friendships, they can't imagine anything ever going wrong. But things often do go wrong, so you need to think about how to manage a potential conflict or breakup. A partnership agreement is like a business prenuptial agreement, and every partnership needs one. The agreement should establish how the partnership can be managed or dissolved if the partners no longer agree on the direction of the business.

Like the sole proprietorship, a partnership is a "pass-through entity." Partners receive a partnership return—IRS Form 1065—which is filed with each partner's personal income tax return. Profits and losses from the business are reported via this form.

The key points of a partnership are:

- No formal filing requirements.

- A partnership agreement is recommended, setting forth rights and responsibilities.

- No protection from personal liability; partners are responsible for the acts of others.

Corporation

When you hear the word "corporation," you probably think of big organizations. But a corporation doesn't have to be big. In fact, a corporation can consist of a single shareholder. A corporation is a legal structure that is separate from its owner(s), which is very different from the sole proprietorship and partnership structures.

Because a corporation is a separate entity, as the owner you are generally protected from personal liability. There *are* exceptions to personal liability protection, which you should discuss with your attorney. As a rule of thumb, however, if you maintain the requisite corporate formalities defined by the statutes of the state in which you incorporate, you most likely will have protection.

Protection from personal liability is the major reason business owners choose to incorporate their businesses. Should your business be unable to pay its debts, unless you've signed personal guarantees your creditors can go after assets of the company, not your personal assets or those of any other shareholders.

To establish a corporation, you must file an Articles of Incorporation document in your state. You also need to create bylaws for the company, issue shares of stock, maintain a corporate record book, and file annual registration forms with the secretary of state's office in the state of incorporation. In most cases, you must establish a board of directors and elect officers. (Check your state statutes, as state requirements vary.) There are expenses associated with establishing a corporation, which you will avoid if you choose a sole proprietorship or partnership. And I strongly recommend hiring an attorney or CPA to guide you through the incorporation process. Once again, it's okay to begin the process on your own, if you prefer, but rely on the expertise of an attorney or CPA to ensure everything is done correctly.

There are two popular types of corporations for small businesses, both of which offer personal liability protection, but have different tax consequences. A "C" corporation is taxed as a separate entity, files its own tax return, and is taxed at a corporate rate. An "S" corporation doesn't file a separate return or pay taxes itself; all profits and losses pass through to the shareholders, who are assessed taxes at their individual income tax rate. Shareholders of an "S" corporation receive an 1120S Schedule K–1 form, which is filed with their personal income tax return.

Most small-business owners prefer to be an "S" corporation because it avoids what is commonly known as the "double taxation" trap. That means a corporation's income can be taxed twice—once when it's earned on the corporate level and again when it's paid to you, the shareholder, in dividends.

Initially, the "S" corporation may seem to you like the logical choice. But if your goal is to attract investors, the "S" corporation has limitations. Consult with an attorny or tax professional before you decide which type of corporation is best for you. The considerations are complicated and it's often costly to change down the road.

Points to keep in mind about a corporation:

- Articles of Incorporation must be filed with the state; each state charges a fee for the filing.

- Corporation must be kept in good standing by filing annual registration reports.

- There must be a board of directors and the corporation must have officers.

- There must be bylaws and documentation of annual meetings of shareholders and board of directors. (Check your state statutes.)

- Shareholders are generally not subject to personal liability.

Limited Liability Company

A limited liability company (LLC) is a type of legal structure that is attractive to many new business owners because it minimizes the risk of personal liability without involving corporate formalities. To form an LLC you must file Articles of Organization (which are similar to Articles of Incorporation) with the appropriate state agency and pay a filing fee. Instead of bylaws, an LLC has what is known as an operating agreement. Once again, while there are websites that provide templates and forms for drafting operating agreements, the content is boilerplate, which may not be appropriate for your business. Therefore, it is advisable to work with a professional to ensure the agreement is written appropriately for your business needs.

Unlike corporations, LLCs are not bound by formal corporate governance requirements. Consisting of members rather than shareholders, LLCs don't issue stock. They are not required to elect officers, hold board meetings, or keep corporate records. Nor is there a requirement to file an annual registration report with the state's secretary of state office.

An LLC may be taxed like an "S" corporation as a pass-through entity, but the LLC is not bound by many of the restrictions that accompany "S" corporation status. For example, an "S" corporation may not have more than 100 shareholders, all of whom must be U.S. citizens or residents. However, any type of person or entity may become a member of an LLC, which is beneficial if you plan to attract investment capital.

Points to keep in mind about a limited liability company are:

- Must file Articles of Organization and pay filing fees to the state.

- Members are generally not subject to personal liability.

- Fewer legal formalities than corporations; no annual filings or meetings required.

- An operating agreement is recommended.

- LLCs are typically pass-through entities.

• • •

Again, consult with a professional adviser such as a CPA or attorney to make sure you choose the appropriate structure for your business.

Federal Employer Identification Number

Once you have established your business structure, you may need to obtain a Federal Employer Identification Number (EIN). Basically, an EIN is your company's Social Security number. It has nothing to do with whether or not you have employees. Every business needs an EIN unless you are a sole proprietorship, or in some states a single-member LLC, in which case you use your Social Security for tax purposes.

It's easy to apply for your EIN. You can obtain the IRS Form SS-4 online (www.irs.gov) and mail or fax it in. But the easiest way of all is to use the IRS phone-in system, which enables you to get your number the same day: (800) 829-4933.

Intellectual Property

The term "intellectual property" involves a lot of different things regarding your business, from trademarks and copyrights to patents. Some types of intellectual property are much easier to protect and manage than others, but regardless of the nature of your company's intellectual property, it is a valuable asset and you absolutely must make sure you protect it.

Imagine starting your business under one name and then learning someone else has launched a similar business using the same name and that person has successfully acquired a trademark for the name as well. You may not have to change the name of your business because you are protected by what's known as "prior usage" (meaning you were using the name prior to its being trademarked). However, if you decide to expand, you most likely will have to do so with a differnt name, particularly if using your current name causes confusion in the marketplace.

Therefore, it's wise to think about protecting your intellectual property early on in your business start-up. The following are some common matters pertainting to intellectual property. This certainly won't cover everything you would need to know, and because this is a complex area of law, you should consult with an attorney who specializes in intellectual property.

Trademarks

What is a trademark? Quite simply, a trademark is your brand. It can include your company name, logo design, tagline, or a combination of all of these things that represent your business. A trademark is unique to your business. One misconception in the market is that you can copyright your business name; that's not true because copyrights do not apply to business names. (Copyright is explained later in this chapter.)

Prior to choosing a name for your business, it's always a good idea to do a name search to make sure no one has already obtained a trademark. Don't fall in love with a business name until you have done your due diligence. You can research existing trademarks online for free using the Trademark Electronic Search System database provided by the U.S. Patent and Trademark Office (www .uspto.gov). However, the database information on the site can be confusing and difficult to decipher. So, once again, an attorney who specializes in this area of law is better equipped to make a more accurate determination.

If there is no registered trademark for the business name you want to use and you want to trademark it for your business, you can file a trademark application online using the Trademark Electronic Application System. Fees associated with the application can be paid online by credit card, by establishing a USPTO account, or via electronic funds transfer.

Why register your trademark? If your business is successful, you don't want others benefiting from your business success by opening a similar business and giving it the same name or one that's very similar to your brand. That would confuse customers and cost you potential business. Your brand has tremendous value, and a trademark provides the protection you need.

Do you need an attorney to file a trademark? Technically, you don't. As noted earlier, there are online systems through which you can file for trademark protection yourself. However, you do so at your own peril. The process is not user-friendly, and if you aren't familiar with all the technicalities, you may not provide yourself with the broadest scope of protection. The cost of an attorney's fees up front may be insignificant compared to legal fees down the road.

Consider Poppy Gall and Carolyn Cooke's million-dollar-plus company, Isis, which manufactures a line of outerwear for active women. The company's original name was Juno, but they were hit with a cease-and-desist order because there was a plus-size women's clothing company with the same name. If Poppy and Carolyn had done their due diligence by conducting a trademark search themselves—or better yet, hired an attorney to determine whether there was a conflict—they would have saved $25,000 in subsequent legal and design fees, plus the frustration of having to rebrand their young company.

Once you have obtained a trademark for your business, you must vigorously defend it or it will lose its value. For example, Kleenex is a trademarked brand name; when the name appears on the product or in advertising, the symbol ™ directly follows the name. Yet, think about how many times people use the word "Kleenex" when they mean "facial tissue." That common-language use of a brand name may put the value of the trademark in jeopardy.

One way to police the use of your trademark is to establish search-engine alerts for the brand name. For example, I have alerts for SBTV.com, SBTV, Small Business Television, and ItsYourBiz.com because these are all trademarked. The alerts help me discover infringements of our trademarks. Usually it is a simple process to protect the brand. I send an email or call the offending party, alerting them about the infringement, and the persons or company are very cooperative and stop using the trademarked name.

The biggest challenge in this regard is when the infringement occurs with a non-U.S. company. Unfortunately, a trademark issued by the USPTO does not provide international protection. However, if you plan to do business globally, you may seek registration in other countries by filing an "international application" with the International Bureau of the World Intellectual Property Organization (www.wipo.int). Consult the USPTO website or an experienced intellectual property attorney for more in-depth information about international trademark rights.

Copyrights

A copyright is automatically secured when an original work is created in a tangible form. That means that you don't have to mail yourself a copy of your work for a copyright to attach, and you don't have to register it with the U.S. Copyright Office. Though you can't copyright an idea, once you transfer the idea to a tangible format, then you technically own the copyright to that original work.

You may notice on many published works, such as newscasts, sport broadcasts, newspaper articles, and books, that there is a notice of copyright. While that is not officially required, it is a good idea to include it as a way of protecting yourself. To include a copyright notice on your original work, use the copyright symbol ©, or simply write the word "copyright." Then insert the year of publication or origination and the copyright owner's name. So, for example, my copyright for this book is: © 2012 Susan Wilson Solovic.

Copyright notices can prevent others from using any marketing materials you have created to promote or describe your business. Similarly, you should include the copyright notice for online elements such as a blog, a website, or an e-newsletter. Materials used in seminars to train or educate customers should also include the copyright notice so as to discourage someone else from using your efforts for their benefit.

Because I write many columns and blog posts for a variety of companies and media organizations, I use search-engine tools to alert me if anyone is picking up and using my material. Some people have literally copied my writing and presented it as their own, even though this is an obvious copyright infringement. There are both civil and criminal penalties for copyright violations, and the severity of the penalties depends on the situation.

Finally, though registration with the U.S. Copyright Office is not mandatory for protection, doing so for major works, such as a screenplay or a software program, is still a good idea. Registration provides a public record of your copyright ownership, and you must be registered in order to file a lawsuit for any infringement of your work. You can search registered copyrights and register your own copyright online for as little as $35. There's more information about the scope of copyright protection at the U.S. Copyright Office's website, www.copyright.gov.

Patents

According to the SBA, small businesses generate 13 times more patents per employee than do large companies. Let's face it: Entre - preneurs are innovators, and America provides ample opportunity for people with great ideas to successfully bring them to market. However, for every great idea that succeeds in moving from the mind to the marketplace, there are countless others that never get off the ground.

Although it has never been credited to anyone, one of my favorite quotes says it best: "Everyone who has ever taken a shower has had an idea. It's the person who gets out of the shower, dries off, and does something about it that makes a difference." So if you have a great idea for a product or service in your business, here are the things you need to know at the outset to ensure your idea makes it to market:

1. What types of things are patentable? To patent something, it has to be original. And make sure no one else has beaten you to the punch. Just because you haven't seen it on the market, that doesn't mean someone hasn't already thought of it. For instance, did you know that for every idea you generate, at least 200 people before you have already thought of it? (Of course, that doesn't mean they have acted on their idea, so do your research.)

2. What kinds of patents exist? The three most common types of patents are:

(a) Utility patent: These are issued for the invention of a new and useful process, machine, manufacture or composition of matter, or a new and useful improvement thereof; (b) Design patent: These are issued for new, original, and ornamental designs for an article of manufacture; (c) Plant patent: These are issued for a new and distinct, invented or discovered asexually reproduced plant, including cultivated mutants, hybrids, and newly found seedlings.

3. Does someone already own the patent? Do your research. Before you invest too much time and money in your idea, conduct an Internet search with key words that apply to your product idea and see what pops up. You can also conduct a patent search on the U.S. Patent and Trademark Office website (www.uspto.gov).

4. How do I present my idea? Once you have determined that your product is truly unique, you need to invest in a prototype and conduct market research. You should describe your invention with such completeness that others could make or use it. Also, just like the type of market research you do when you have an idea for a business start-up, you'll need to demonstrate that there is a viable market opportunity for your invention. Are there people out there willing to buy and use the product if it becomes available? Your prototype should help you make that determination and establish the costs associated with bringing the product to market, as well.

5. *How I document my inventive process?* It's important to keep accurate records, so be sure to put all your ideas, notes, and drawings in an inventor's journal, and have it signed, witnessed, and dated. Be careful about disclosing your ideas to others. Make sure you get a confidentiality or nondisclosure document signed before discussing your ideas with others. " 'Be afraid to share your idea' is very good advice," says attorney Chris Kelleher. "The reason being that until you actually file for some type of patent application, if you disclose your idea to anyone else who isn't contractually obligated to keep their mouth shut, then they can use that idea and may be able to beat you to the patent office."

The patent process differs from copyright protection, in that the first patent filed is the one that wins, whereas copyright attaches automatically to a tangible medium as soon as it is created. Also, you should know up front that, for the patent process, patience is not a virtue—it's a necessity. It can take years to complete (literally, *years!*), and it can cost a significant amount of money, depending on the complexity of the patent. So if you're serious about obtaining a patent, dig in and get ready for the long haul.

Do you need an attorney? In this case, the answer is an unequivocal *yes*. There are no shortcuts. The patent process is not forgiving, and if you make a mistake, even in the early stages, you could blow your entire opportunity. Specifically, you'll need an attorney who has experience in filing patents—ideally one with experience in your particular field.

Caution: Avoid the infomercial scams. There are lots of commercials and advertisements for companies that promise to run with your idea and do everything for you. They intimate an easy road to making millions with your invention. But there is no such thing as an easy road to success. To avoid getting scammed, ask for references and success rates. If the representative employs high-pressure sales tactics, that should be a huge red flag. Make sure you understand what the total package of services will cost. If you don't get a clear answer then beware, it's probably a scam.

For every successful invention you see on a product infomercial or QVC, there are thousands and thousands that never got off the ground. History shows that only one out of every 5,000 inventions has a successful product launch. And a very small percentage of these products ever generate a meaningful amount of money for the inventors. In fact, many entrepreneur/inventors with whom I've spoken are still hoping simply to recover their initial investments.

Words to the wise: Ask questions—and move cautiously.

For additional information on obtaining a patent, visit www.uspto.gov, www.uiausa.org, and www.ItsYourBiz.com.

A Handshake Is Nice . . . but Get It in Writing

No matter how well you believe you know someone, or how much you trust someone, when it comes to business, always, *always* get things in writing. Without a written document defining responsibilities and expectations, when something goes wrong, it's just your word against someone else's. That's not a good position to be in, and it's definitely bad business.

Yes, a lot of people say they do business on the honor system. And in an ideal world, I would support that 100 percent. In fact, at times I have operated from that perspective in my own business. But it takes getting burned only once before you realize that it's simply good business practice for all parties involved to formalize your agreement in writing.

I served on a jury for a civil case in which a contractor sued a property owner for money owed on what the contractor referred to as a "contract." The property owner countersued the contractor for reimbursement of money he claimed he had to pay to have the work redone because it was not done according to "contract" specifications. The problem was that neither party had bothered to sign an actual contract, and each had a different version of the same document that they claimed represented an agreement. It was a very boring trial, but in the end the jury did not award anything to either party because neither could prove its claim.

I wished I could have been a television judge hearing this case because I would have ridiculed both parties for their stupidity. The defendant, the property owner, was the proprietor of a paint contracting company, and the plaintiff, the general contractor, said he'd been in business for more than 30 years. Both of them should have known better, and the result of their sloppy business practices cost them a significant amount of money.

You don't always need to incur the expense of a formal contract filled with legal jargon, but you do need to create a document that outlines precisely what each party will do, when it will be done, what the pricing will be, and any other specifics that are necessary for the satisfactory completion of the project.

When working with an outside vendor providing services such as photography, website design, or graphic design, remember to make the contract a work-for-hire agreement. In other words, make sure you own the sole rights to whatever work the vendor does for you. If you don't establish that up front, your rights to the product could be limited. For example, suppose a photo is taken for your company brochure. Without a work-for-hire contract, you may be limited to using the photo for that particular project only. If you use it for anything else, the photographer can argue that, because he owns the copyright, you must pay for any use beyond the scope of the original work.

So get it in writing! Memories are short. Never work with a vendor or a customer without a written agreement. I can't overstate how important this is. The key components of any agreement are:

- An overview of the scope of the work/project

- A list of deliverables

- A start date and completion date (you may also add milestones between the two)

- Ownership of intellectual property rights (e.g., copyright)

- Compensation and payment terms

- Termination provisions (i.e., what happens if either party wants out of the agreement)

CHAPTER 9

---

where will you locate your business?

SOMETIMES THE SUCCESS of your business can be predicated on selecting the right location. For retail stores and restaurants, this is typically the case. However, for the majority of small-business start-ups today, where you launch your business has little bearing on your success. Because of technology, you can start operations in your garage or basement and do business all over the world. You can look as though you are a big business operation while working in a spare bedroom in the comfort of your bathrobe and slippers.

In 1998, when I started what is now called Susan Solovic Media, my office was, in fact, a spare bedroom, and I worked on a card table with cardboard-boxed files and old, discarded furniture. Despite my meager surroundings, people often assumed I was a relatively large company. And today it is even easier to look large without a big budget.

Home-Based Businesses

It wasn't that long ago that, if you operated your business out of your home, you weren't taken seriously. Not so anymore. In the United States, another home-based business starts about every 10 to 15 seconds. In fact, starting a business in your home can be a smart decision because it dramatically minimizes your start-up costs. However, starting a business in your home isn't as easy as finding a space to set up your office. There are special things to consider, including whether you have the right personality for working at home.

The thought of working from home sounds wonderful to people who schlep to the office each day in all kinds of weather, as well as people who grumble about irritating office politics. However, to be a successful at-home worker you need to have a great deal of self-discipline and be comfortable working alone.

Let's start with the morning alarm. When you work for yourself at home, you can set your own hours, so you might think, *Who cares what time I get up and get going?* But the cardinal rule for any home-based business is to schedule work hours and stick with them. That takes discipline.

When you work at home, a host of distractions can keep you from focusing on your business. You may find yourself interrupted frequently by family, neighbors, or friends who don't consider you "at work" because you are home. That's why you should establish ground rules. Make sure other people understand that you have business hours, just like any other professional. Ask them to respect that. One at-home entrepreneur who is married with children created a sign for the door to her office area that said "At work. Do not disturb."

Minimizing the distractions also means you have to ignore common household distractions. You may think, *A load of laundry should take only a few minutes. . . . A quick trip to the grocery store shouldn't take that long. . . . Picking up the living room and running the vacuum isn't a big deal. . . . I'll just watch a few innings of that game. . . .* Before you know it, the day has gone by and you haven't accomplished much, if anything, relating to your business. When I work at home, ignoring household chores is easy. (I don't like doing them.) But for some people, seeing things around the house that need to be done can drive them crazy. If that's the case for you, then you either need to find another work location or discipline yourself to look the other way.

Background noise is another potential problem for a home-based business. The sound of barking dogs and crying children won't make you appear professional. If you have young children, you may need to consider day care. As for pets, make sure they are someplace where their activity won't interfere with business. I'm fortunate. I have a shih tzu who never barks. When I work at home, he lays by my feet and never makes a sound. He is an excellent co-worker. (So much so I've given him a title. He is "chairman of the bone.")

If you're a home-based entrepreneur, you'll also need to make sure the area you use for your business is *dedicated* to your business—especially if you want to take the home-based business tax credit. For example, your computer should be used for business use only, and not loaded with video games, vacation photos, or other personal items. Even if your workspace is in a joint use room, you should carve out a business-related area that is off limits to anyone else living in your home.

In addition, make sure home-based businesses are allowed in your neighborhood and/or building. Check the zoning laws for your community. Some municipalities prohibit home-based businesses, or require special permits for their operation. And many subdivisions, condominium associations, apartment buildings, and cooperatives don't allow home-based businesses.

If you own your home, check with your insurance agent to determine whether your homeowners policy covers a home-based business. You need to make sure that if you experience a fire, theft, or a natural disaster, any losses connected with your business will be covered. Also, if you plan to have customers, clients, or employees coming to your home, check to make sure your policy covers you should someone be injured while in your home for business purposes; you may need additional liability coverage.

When you're a home-based business owner, it is easy to feel isolated. Some people are okay with that, but others find it stifling. The lack of interaction may even be depressing for some. Plan to get out of your office and go to lunch with other business owners, vendors, or clients. Sign up for a seminar. Go to a networking event. Take a break and head to the gym. Interacting with others and getting a change of scenery will keep your creative juices flowing and increase your productivity. Many small-business owners use their local coffee shop as a second office. Today, many of these venues offer wireless connections and allow customers to stay for as long as they like. Personally, I spent many work hours at coffee shops before I had an actual office.

If you operate your business out of your home, think seriously about using a postal box for your mail rather than your home address, particularly if you live alone. In these crazy times, you never know what people are thinking. The same is true about inviting customers, clients, vendors, and even employees into your home. Make sure you know them well and feel comfortable opening your home to them.

Unfortunately, vendors, customers, and even employees can steal personal property from your home. Just be smart about how you conduct your business.

Alternatives to Commercial Office Space

The cost of renting office space when you are just starting your business can be significant—a major financial commitment. But there are some options for filling the gap between a home-based operation and a full-fledged commercial office space.

• *Bartering.* In recent years, many companies have downsized and, as a result, often have vacant offices. In some cases, new business owners can barter for that office space. They take an open office in someone else's company and, in exchange for rent, provide services or products to that business.

• *Incubators.* A small-business incubator is a facility that offers adaptable office space and support services at a discounted rate. They are designed to accelerate the successful development of start-ups. Incubators differ in the way they deliver their services and in the types of clients they serve, but the success rate of companies that graduate from an incubator program greatly exceeds that of the general market. Part of the reason may be that, in order to be accepted into an incubator program, your business idea is reviewed first for viability. You can learn more about programs in your area from the National Business Incubator Association (www.nbia.org).

• *Executive office suites.* Business centers or executive office suites can be a turnkey solution for your office space needs. These companies provide fully equipped offices that you share with other businesses and utilize on an as-needed basis. It is a good option for precluding the isolation and loneliness of always working from home, and can also provide a better place to meet clients. Some companies use these executive office suites just to have a prestigious address. For example, an advertising agency with which I did some business had an upscale address in New York, on Madison Avenue. It turned out that the agency was really located in New Jersey and used the Madison Avenue executive office suite location for its mailing address.

In addition to the office space, executive office centers provide conference rooms that can be rented when needed. Plus, the staff is available to handle mail services, clerical support, and telephones. I've used executive centers when I've been on the road and needed a landline, Internet connection, and office space for meetings. This arrangement certainly beats meeting in a hotel lobby or restaurant.

Using shared office space also gives you the opportunity to collaborate with other business owners and professionals. Depending on who the other users of the space are, you may find an opportunity to partner on projects or barter for services.

If you want to use an executive office center as a long-term solution, the operating company will require you to sign a contract. Usually there is a three-month minimum, which is much better than the five- or ten-year lease most commercial landlords require. Regardless of the option you choose, it is a good idea to have your attorney review any rental agreement before you sign.

To find the best office arrangement, shop around. You want something that is conveniently located for your primary customers or clients. You also want to be in a building with businesses that complement your own. Don't be too intimidated by a sales agent who tries to force you to make a quick decision—and always negotiate the price. Also, don't forget to ask your business advisers, mentors, and other business owners for their opinions about the space and rental terms.

Choosing a Commercial Office

For some types of new businesses, owners feel the need to be located in commercial office space. For example, lawyers often prefer to start their practices in a commercial space. As your business grows, you may find it advantageous to make the leap from home-based to commercial space.

Before you choose rental office space, carefully review your actual needs. How much space do you require? What type of building would be best suited for your needs? Strip mall? Small office building? High-rise? Do you need a prestigious address? Do you need or want foot traffic? How much can you afford to spend on a monthly basis? Is ample parking nearby important? Once you have determined your needs, contact a commercial realtor in your area. A commercial realtor will know what space will fit your needs and which facilities fall within your price range.

Personally, I think hunting for office space is a lot like house hunting. It's easy to fall in love with something that's beyond your means. So keep your eyes focused on your business objectives and don't be lured by luxuries you don't need and can't afford in these early stages of your business. Most start-up companies I've seen, including my own, began in lower-end buildings. Funds were used to grow the business, not supply the prestige.

Once you've found the space you want, you need to negotiate the terms of the lease. There's a lot of information you'll have to obtain beyond just the basic cost per square foot. Here are some questions you should ask:

• *What is the term of the lease?* You need to know this so you can decide whether you are comfortable committing to the space for that length of time. For example, let's say the term of the lease is ten years, but you think your business will double in size during that time; don't sign the ten-year lease unless you know that there is space into which you can expand.

- *Will my rent increase?* Some leases include provisions for rent increases. You need to know how large the increases will be and when they will occur.

- *Who is responsible for the utilities, taxes, trash disposal, snow removal, and general maintenance, such as the HVAC and plumbing?* If you are responsible for any of these, they will be additional overhead for your business.

- *What is the current condition of the space?* Is it satisfactory the way it is, or does it need to be painted and updated? Who is responsible for that? Many landlords will include a certain amount of what is called "build-out" when they rent space. Find out what the landlord is willing to do.

- *Will I have to guarantee the lease?* For a relatively new business owner, most likely the landlord will require a personal guarantee for the lease. That means that, even if you go out of business, you will be personally responsible for the ongoing rent unless you are able to sublet the space per terms of the lease.

Most important, before you sign a lease, make sure the rental amount is in line with rents of other properties in the area. A friend of mine was leasing new space for a hair salon, and the lease did not provide for trash removal. While negotiating the lease, he decided to walk around the property and talk with some of the other tenants. In doing so, he learned that the landlord covered trash removal for the other renters. You must do your homework to make sure you get the best deal for your business.

When Location Really Matters

For retail businesses and restaurants, as mentioned earlier in this chapter, location is crucial. A wrong choice can make or break the business. That's why many franchise organizations and big chains spend many thousands of dollars on research to choose the right locations. But without that kind of information, how do you choose the best location?

First, when you look at a vacant location, find out what types of businesses were there before, and for how long. I'm sure you've seen certain buildings that have housed restaurant after restaurant, and nothing seems to make it. Chances are it is a bad location for a restaurant. So analyze the location and figure out what about it made the previous businesses fail (or succeed); it's probably something you cannot change.

Find out about turnover in the building itself. Are the other tenants long-term renters? You don't want to be in a space where there are continual vacancies. Not only is that not good for business but also it may indicate a problem with the landlord or the building.

It may seem obvious, but be sure to see whether any of your competitors are in the area. There is no need to increase your business challenges by opening close to one of your competitors unless you think you can capture some of their customers, like the fast-food chains tend to do. Also, pay careful attention to what other types of businesses are in the area. You don't want to open a high-end clothing store in a retail center with a hardware store, discount shoe store, and video rental center, for instance. It is preferable to be in a location where the customer base of other businesses complements your target market.

• • •

With your place of business settled, you're ready to move on to another major consideration—finance. The next chapter will help you take your business from a humble beginning to much greater heights.

CHAPTER 10

---

from humble beginnings to great enterprises

"I'VE GOT A GREAT idea for a business, but I don't have any money to get it started! Where can I go to get money from the government or find investors to help me start my business?"

If I had a dime for every time I've been asked this question, I'd be wealthy enough to establish my own small-business loan company. Almost every person with a start-up business idea wishes he or she had start-up money—or more money. In fact, many people use their lack of funds as an excuse for not starting their business. Here's what I tell them: You must not really want to go into business.

Entrepreneurs know how to do a lot with very little. Some of the biggest brand names today had humble beginnings and started with very little capital. They didn't go to the bank. They didn't seek free money from the government. Most of them didn't even tap their family and friends. They used their innovative minds, their meager personal resources, and a lot of sweat equity to get their businesses off the ground.

When Steve Jobs and Steve Wozniak decided to launch Apple Computer in January 1977, Jobs sold his VW bus and Wozniak his HP scientific calculator to raise their initial investment of $1,300. And as they say, the rest is history.

I've met entrepreneurs who have sold family jewelry, cars, and even household furnishings to raise money for their business ventures. One woman minimized her start-up expenses by bartering her company's services in exchange for a fully equipped office. Where there's a will there's a way. In fact, most small businesses start with less than $10,000 in capital. How is this possible? Because technology has driven down substantially the cost of starting and operating a business, so it doesn't take barrelfuls of cash to get your company rolling. Don't get discouraged if you think you'll need a load of money to start your company. If you've estimated your start-up expenses and it's more than you can raise on your own, then you may just have to scale back. You can start on a part-time basis and grow your business in phases, but you can still get there.

Break Open Your Piggy Bank

When it comes to finding funds for your business, you might as well go to your piggy bank as to any other bank. My personal estimation is that over 75 percent of start-up funds are raised from personal assets and what's known as family-friendly funding—money loaned or invested by family and friends. But when it comes to the early start-up funds, the best place to look is in your own pocket. Look under the sofa cushions. Check your pockets. Dig through old handbags and wallets. Break open your piggy bank. Forgo that daily latte and instead set aside the money for your business start-up.

Ideally, you should begin saving money for your business start-up in advance, but that's not always an option. So when you create your business plan and estimate your start-up costs, be prepared to begin with a bare-bones launch. There's nothing wrong with scaling back your idea and starting smaller than you had originally planned. A part-time job can help you manage your cash flow while you get the business up and running. (Yes, I realize that's difficult, but no one said starting a business would be easy.)

But, in addition to the piggy bank, here are some other financing options to consider.

Your Home Equity

Up until recently, a lot of start-ups used home equity loans as a financing source. Home equity loans are granted based on your creditworthiness—the home owner's—and the amount of equity in your property. *Equity* is the difference between the balance of the mortgage and the market value of the home—what banks call the *loan-to-value* ratio. So if you owe a lot on your home and the market in your area has dropped, as is the case for many people in today's economy, an equity loan most likely won't be an option. Banks generally provide home equity loans in two forms: a traditional lump-sum loan amount or as a revolving line of credit.

Even when the economy turns around, be careful about how much equity you use for your start-up. Because starting a business is risky, there is a high probability that you will lose the money you invest in your business. You don't want to go into debt for more money than you can afford to repay.

Retirement Savings

Many people's second most valuable asset is their 401(k) plan or other retirement fund. Depending on your age, when you started investing, and how the market has affected your portfolio, you could have a nice chunk of change sitting there. It's easy to be tempted to use it for your business start-up; but before you even consider whether it's possible and/or practical to drain that resource, think about your life stage. The older you are, the harder it is to replace your retirement nest egg. And I'm not making a political statement when I point out that there's no guarantee that Social Security or Medicare will be available when you retire. Plus, it is nearly impossible to live on Social Security alone. The question for you: Is the gamble worth it? Most experts would say it is ill-advised to use these funds, but thousands of new entrepreneurs are resorting to this type of funding; the choice is yours.

That being said, if you determine you want to use your personal retirement funds, you'll have various options, depending on the type of plan you have. If you've got a 401(k) plan, check with the plan administrator to see whether loans are allowed for business purposes. If so, the IRS permits borrowing against 401(k) plans without your having to pay taxes or a penalty on the amount borrowed. However, if you have an IRA, you can borrow against it, but only for 60 days. If you repay it one day late, you'll owe taxes, and depending on your age, perhaps penalties as well.

Participants in a 403(B) plan can also borrow against the policy. The IRS allows up to 50 percent of the participant's vested value, to a maximum of $50,000. However, the plans require you to repay the loan within a specified period of time, and if you leave your employer, you either have to repay the full amount or have the balance considered a taxable distribution to you.

There is one extremely complicated mechanism that some start-ups use, and that's one that allows you to invest your retirement savings in your business, as opposed to borrowing against it. It requires establishing a corporation, creating a corporate retirement account with that new company, and rolling your existing retirement funds into that account. Funds are then invested in the stock of your new corporation. Again, this is extremely complex, and it requires the expertise of a professional CPA, investment counselor, or attorney. Some experts warn that this falls within the gray area of the law, so proceed with caution.

Credit Cards

Credit cards are a popular and convenient means of financing a small-business start-up. A 2009 survey from the National Small Business Association (NSBA) showed that most businesses use credit cards to help with business financing. Of the businesses responding, 5 percent used an SBA loan, 19 percent used no financing in the past year, and 59 percent said they had utilized credit cards for their capital needs. Seventy-seven percent of the respondents said they used more than one credit card, and 23 percent used four or more.

You don't necessarily need to open a new business credit card account for your start-up. In fact, in most cases, the rates for business credit cards are higher than for consumer cards. (Business credit cards are advantageous, however, as your business grows.) My advice is to designate one or more of the consumer credit cards you've already got now for business use only. For record-keeping purposes, it's important not to mingle your business and personal expenses.

While utilizing credit cards for business can be expensive, it doesn't have to be. Watch for cards offering zero percent introductory rates. These can save you money because you have use of the funds without interest usually for one year. Also, use the online tools that let you compare rates, fees, and benefits of multiple cards so you can choose the best card for your needs. Remember, many cards give customer rewards, so think about what type of reward would be most beneficial for your new company. Cash back? Airline miles? General reward points?

Credit cards can be a lifeline for a small business. A number of years ago, my friend Janell started a business doing commercial window tinting. She landed a major commercial contract during her first year and took it to the bank to establish a line of credit so she could buy inventory and manage payroll during the project. The bank turned her down cold. So she maxed out her credit cards, along with those of other members of her family, to complete the contract; then she paid the outstanding balance as soon as she was paid by her client.

If you are confused about which card to use, check out Cardratings.com (www.cardratings.com). The site reviews credit cards from all major issuers as well as from many regional banks and credit unions. If you are interested in a business credit card, Credit Donkey provides free comparisons of business credit cards. You can search, compare, and even apply online at www.credit donkey.com/business.

Tapping Family and Friends for Financing

Mixing money and relationships is, at best, a mixed bag. The Limited, one of my favorite trendy clothing stores, was started in 1963 by Leslie Wexner, who borrowed $5,000 from his aunt to open a small women's retail shop called Leslie's Limited. The Limited now operates in thousands of cities across the United States and boasts revenues in the billions. So, yes, there are a number of success stories that involved family financing. However, there are many sad tales as well.

Raising start-up or growth capital from family and friends—
private investors—is not uncommon. But neither are the lawsuits
and destroyed relationships that occur as a result. I'm not a fan of
TV shows such as *Judge Judy*, but because my dad lives with me
and enjoys watching them, I have caught a few episodes. Many of
the programs deal with money issues among family and friends.
One party says it was a loan, and the other party says it was a gift.
Or even worse, the defending party denies having received the
money in the first place. Quite simply, the potential for castastro-
phe is enormous.

Most of these financial problems occur because the transactions
were handled poorly. Therefore, to avoid a relationship disaster,
before seeking funds from family and friends, do the necessary
preparation—it is vital. You need to approach a family/friend loan
as professionally as you would any other source of funding. Be prepared with your business plan and a professional presentation.
Demonstrate to your potential investors that you have a well-
thought-out plan with defensible strategies and projections.

Before you begin dialing for dollars, make a list of potential
investors: people you know, including family, friends, and business
associates. At this stage, don't worry about whether you think they'll
be interested; simply make the list.

Once you have your list, you can narrow it down. Here are some
things to consider:

- *Affluence.* Can this person afford to lose the money? Keep
  in mind the high degree of risk involved in investing in a
  small business, and consider the individual's financial
  well-being.

- *Business experience.* The best investor is someone who
  understands the entrepreneurial process and can evaluate
  your business opportunity. Often successful entrepreneurs

172 / IT'S YOUR BIZ

are interested in learning about new ventures and helping new businesses succeed.

- *Emotional baggage.* Avoid approaching someone with whom you have had conflict in the past. A precarious relationship could lead to problems in your business. Additionally, don't ask someone who may have to deal with repercussions from others in the event he or she loans you money. For example, a spouse who might become angry about the investment could create serious problems, and you don't need more issues to deal with when you're trying to get your business off the ground.

Once you have your list of top potential investors, schedule meetings with them to discuss the opportunity. (Don't ambush them and ask for the cash at a cocktail party or family gathering.) After you meet with them and review your plan, give them time to digest the information and think it over. Never put pressure on anyone to make an immediate decision. Ask them when would be a good time to follow up, and make sure you do.

Be careful about getting your hopes up just because someone agrees to meet with you. People will often say "no" regardless of their feelings toward you. Don't take it personally. There may be issues in their lives of which you aren't aware, and those may make them uncomfortable loaning or investing at this time. Never get angry or make someone feel guilty, and don't resort to emotional blackmail. Maintain your integrity. Things may change and you never know when you might need to approach someone again in the future.

Keep It Legal: Get It in Writing

If you find someone who agrees to lend you money for your business, you'll need one critical legal document to formalize the arrangement: a promissory note. Many people, because of their relationship with you, will tell you that it's not necessary. At the time of the initial loan, they feel good about being able to help you, so they are comfortable giving you the funds without any documentation. Not smart! It is for your protection as well as theirs that the loan is properly documented. People have short memories.

You can find templates for promissory notes online or in office supply stores. Basically, the promissory note identifies both the borrower and the lender by name, states that the lender has given the borrower a specific amount of money, sets out the repayment terms of the loan, and requires the borrower's signature.

You will need to negotiate an appropriate interest rate for the loan repayment terms. A good place to start is using the Applicable Federal Rate (AFR) as your base. The AFR is set by the IRS as a minimum for private loans, and if you use anything less, the IRS will consider the difference between your rate and the AFR to be a gift and will impute interest on it, putting your lender at risk for gift-tax liability. The rate changes monthly, but can be found on the IRS website. Just type "AFR" into the website's search engine.

Because the AFR is very low, your lender may want a higher interest rate. What's the appropriate rate? Good question. That's where you'll need to negotiate. Most institutional investors want a higher return because of the substantial risk they are taking by investing their money in a start-up. But because you have a personal relationship with the lender, that's probably not going to be the case. However, it's a good idea to suggest an interest rate that will make the loan an attractive transaction for the lender. For example, if someone has money in CDs earning a very low interest rate, you could offer a higher rate for the use of those funds, which could make it an attractive investment option.

Most money from family and friends is in the nature of unsecured loans; however, you should be prepared to offer your lender collateral. Make a list of the personal assets you have that could secure the loan.

To establish a loan repayment schedule, you can utilize loan calculators on sites such as Bankrate.com. Decide when you will start repaying the loan and what, if any, penalties there may be for late payments or prepayment of the loan.

Depending on the sum you're trying to raise for your business, you may need to consult with an attorney, as there may be state or federal regulations governing the transaction. Also, an attorney or CPA can advise you about any tax liabilities that you may incur.

Commercial Loans and Lenders

So you want to go to a bank for your financing, either now or in the future. It's never too early to strike up a relationship with people in the financial community. Get to know people in the business by attending networking events and programs for small-business owners. Just as with any type of business dealing, it's easier to get in the door when you already know someone.

Doing the Groundwork

Remember, banks don't make loans—people do. So if you establish a relationship with a banker, you'll have an advocate on your side. Even if the bankers you know aren't the right ones to help you with your financing needs, they are good referral sources and can potentially assist you in identifying financing options.

It's also important to know that, when it comes to making small-business loans, not all banks are created equal. You need a bank that is active in the market and is creative about putting deals together. Ask for recommendations and introductions from other businesses in your area. Your local SBA office may have recommendations as well, and on the SBA website there's a lender tool kit to help small-business owners identify SBA lenders in their communities.

In addition to identifying those banks with a small-business orientation, you need to know whether the bank lends to businesses in your particular industry. For example, a bank may have gotten burned by too many loan defaults in the construction industry, so it may not be open to loan applications in that field right now. If you're in construction and you know that going in, you won't waste your time.

It's also a smart idea for your business to establish a banking relationship prior to submitting a loan application. This means that you'll need to find a bank that offers the types of services you'll want for your business. The size of the bank isn't as important as the relationship you can develop with it. In fact, small community banks today are stepping up to the plate and becoming excellent resources for small businesses.

If you don't need a loan right away, try to establish some credit history for your new venture anyway. The bank might provide a small credit line with a personal guarantee that you could use and pay back quickly. Demonstrating the creditworthiness of your company will be helpful down the road if and when you apply for a business loan.

Your Friendly Local Banker—Not Always So Friendly

The funny thing about banks is that they are happy to loan you money when you don't need it, but when you do need it, they're not so eager. It has gotten even tougher to get a loan since the recent economic downturn. A July 2010 report from the National Small Business Association found that 41 percent of respondents said they couldn't get adequate financing. That number was up from 22 percent from just two years ago.

Banks have very strict underwriting standards and guidelines. So for a start-up company with no credit history, or a small business that is struggling financially, it is nearly impossible to obtain financing from a bank—even a loan backed by the Small Business Administration (more on SBA loans later). So be prepared to hear a lot of "no"s.

As with any type of financing source, bankers need to review and analyze your business plan. Bankers don't make quick judgments, so the process can take considerable time. If you haven't done a good job of crunching the numbers, this is when you'll pay the price. Loan officers may not completely understand your business, but they understand numbers, and you won't be able to fool them. Bankers see numerous business plans and they know what makes sense and what doesn't.

Because you won't have any historical data for your business, you'll need to convince the bank officer that you and/or your team have the right experience to start and grow this venture. You'll need to be specific about the types of experience and success you've enjoyed, and how they apply to your ability to build your new business.

Also, banks look for a financial commitment from you, the owner. There is no way around it. You should be prepared to invest in your own business. No bank is going to loan you 100 percent of the money you need; and while the amount varies, you probably won't be able to get a loan for more than 50 percent of what you actually need.

The bank needs to know what collateral you have available in case you default on the loan. Collateral is property or personal belongings that are pledged to the lending source to secure the interest in the loan. Every loan program, even "microloan" programs, requires some form of collateral to secure the loan.

Don't be discouraged if you initially get rejected. Many successful entrepreneurs heard "no" many times before they finally got a "yes." Keep in mind that a "no" answer doesn't necessarily mean "never." Get past the "no" and listen to the reasons the loan request was denied. Sometimes simple adjustments in your loan package, such as more personal investment, additional collateral, or revised projections, may be all it takes to close the deal.

Small Business Administration Loans

A common misconception among new business owners is that the SBA is an agency with money to loan to small businesses. The truth is that, in most situations, the SBA does not make direct loans; rather, it guarantees loans made by banks and other lenders as a means to encourage small-business lending. Therefore, to obtain an SBA-backed loan you must go through the loan application process and review with a financial institution.

The most popular SBA loan program for small businesses is the 7(a) program. It is available for a variety of general business purposes and is designated for both start-up and existing businesses. In addition to the 7(a) loan program, the SBA has other programs for microloans, export loans, disaster assistance, and long-term loans for fixed assets such as real estate. The SBA website provides a complete listing of all of its programs (www.sba.gov).

Other Sources of Money

Money may not grow on trees, but there's more out there, available to you, if you look beyond the obvious and traditional sources.

Peer-to-Peer Lending

With the increasing popularity of social-networking sites, we've seen a new type of lending emerge on the Internet—peer-to-peer lending. These sites are similar to dating sites: They match people who want to borrow money with people who have money to lend.

Currently, two of the most popular sites are Lending Club and Prosper (www.lendingclub.com and www.prosper.com, respectively). Lending Club says it replaces the high cost and complexity of bank lending with a faster, smarter way to borrow and invest. Prosper notes that it allows people to invest in each other in a way that is financially and socially rewarding.

Both sites boast impressive results. As of this writing, Prosper's website claims it has over one million members and has funded over $208 million in loans. At Lending Club, loans funded to date were $173,271,375.

Crowd-Funding

Another innovative approach to small-business funding is what has become known as crowd-funding. Would-be entrepreneurs pitch their ideas on a variety of crowd-funding websites, and people who belong to the site's online network can decide whether or not they'd like to donate to the concept. Yes, I do mean donate. As of this writing, the Securities and Exchange Commission (SEC) does not permit these sites to provide an ownership interest—or equity stake—in the business ventures; however, it is in the process of reviewing its decision, so that may soon change.

Crowd-funding emerged about a decade ago as a way for artists, filmmakers, and musicians to raise donations from a community of online supporters. The idea has now spread to small businesses, which have watched traditional financing sources dry up in the past couple of years. IndieGoGo.com, ProFounder.com, and PeerBackers.com are a few of the most popular sites. There is no charge to post your business idea; however, the site makes money by taking a small percentage of the funds raised.

Microloans

For start-ups or small businesses looking for growth capital, microloans are another popular funding source. Microloans are just as the name describes: small amounts of money, generally under $35,000. Typically, microloan borrowers are categorized as pre-bankable—meaning their companies aren't strong enough to obtain traditional bank loans. The loans are provided by private, public, and nonprofit organizations. For example, the SBA makes funds available to certain designated lenders (nonprofit community-based organizations with experience in lending), as well as management and technical assistance. These organizations in turn make the microloans to eligible borrowers.

While the most well-known microloan programs are likely in the United States, the concept did not originate in America. Rather, it originated in Bangladesh as a way to combat poverty. In fact, the economist who devised the program, Muhammad Yunus, won the Nobel Peace Prize in 2006. Given this history, people often refer to a microloan as a "poor loan." Although microloans are made to people and businesses that are not considered bankable, their success rates are impressive. If you'd like to learn more, read the excellent and inspiring book *Banker to the Poor* by Alan Jolis, which tells the story of Muhammad Yunus and his program. It illustrates what a tremendous impact one person can have on the world.

While microloans are generally easier to obtain than conventional loans, business owners who apply for them must provide a sufficient guarantee that the loan will be paid back through cash flow, collateral, or a reasonable amount of personal credit. To find a microloan program in your area, check with your local Chamber of Commerce or economic development council.

Grants

The idea of "free money" is seductive. Many small-business owners ask me about how to obtain a grant to start their businesses.

For the most part, there is no such thing as free money. Grants are difficult and time-consuming to obtain, although not impossible. Typically, grants are available only for specific types of businesses or particular economic initiatives. Grants.gov is a good place to find and apply for federal grants. However, check with your state and local governments as well.

Angel Investors

An angel investor is someone who invests in a business venture by providing capital for a start-up or expansion. But don't be fooled by the name. They aren't necessarily benevolent people doling out cash to needy businesses. They are typically affluent individuals who are willing to invest in high-risk, start-up business ventures in return for equity (ownership in your business) and a high return on their investment.

Generally, small businesses turn to angel capital after they've exhausted their personal resources and "family-friendly" funding. According to the Center for Venture Research, during the first half of 2010, total investments made by angel investors were $8.5 billion. About 25,200 entrepreneurial ventures were funded.

How do you find these so-called angels? Today, more and more individual investors are joining angel investment groups. The Angel Capital Association is an excellent resource to help you locate such a group (angelcapitalassociation.org). Also, the Angel Capital Education Foundation provides information, seminars, and resources to help you learn about the angel investment process.

Learn as much as you can before you begin your quest for angel funding. Angel investors tend to invest in ideas and individuals who show passion and a strong desire to succeed. But enthusiasm alone won't put money in the bank. Angels also expect you to present a solid, realistic business plan. They're looking for good financials along with high-growth potential. Finally, if the angel invests in your business, he or she is going to hold you accountable for producing results, and will most likely want a seat on your board of directors.

Venture Capital

Of all the types of business funding, venture capital is the least understood, and it is not for the meek. Venture capital—also known as VC—is a type of equity financing typically used for high-risk and high-growth companies. A typical VC investment is for five to seven years, and the investor will expect a return on the money either from the sale of the business or by offering to sell shares in the company to the public, which is known as an initial public offering (IPO). Unless you have already owned a successful venture-backed company, it is highly unlikely you'll be able to attract venture capital for a new start-up.

When a VC firm invests in a company, it receives a percentage of ownership in that company. The percentage depends on how large the investment is. Of course, a venture capitalist who decides to invest in your company isn't about to hand you a check and walk away until it's time to cash in. Rather, the VC will expect to have some control over your business.

The amount of control a venture capital firm will expect to wield varies. Depending on the size of the investment, a venture firm generally requires one or two of your company's board seats to be filled by its members. It also often seeks to protect its investment by actively overseeing the management of your company and requiring that certain fundamental business decisions receive its prior approval. In some respects, instead of being the captain of your own ship, with VC funds you'll find yourself "reporting" to a board of directors that will hold you accountable and expect results. Many entrepreneurs who are mavericks by nature bristle at the thought.

Worse yet, a venture capital investor may decide you aren't the right person to serve in the CEO role! The VC firm may want to replace you with someone it believes is more experienced. Pascal Levensohn, the founder and managing director of Levensohn Venture Partners, a San Francisco-based early-stage venture capital firm that manages $200 million in assets across three funds, says most venture-backed companies experience at least one chief executive officer change as they evolve from a start-up to a fully integrated company. Typically, this situation occurs when the VC firm believes the founder does not have the operational skills to grow the company. For most company founders, that's a difficult pill to swallow. Even when you know going into the deal that it's a possibility, if it actually happens it can be traumatic. In some instances, the founder not only loses the CEO title but also gets fired from his or her own company!

But venture capital funds can spur major growth in companies. Think of many of the big names such as Google, Facebook, and Twitter; all have grown with VC funds. Whether or not it's right for your business depends on one critical question: Do you want all of a small pie or a small piece of a really big pie? It's up to you.

The Perfect Pitch: Knowing How to Present

When you're on the money hunt, whether you're pitching to family and friends, bankers, or equity investors such as angels or VCs, you need to know how to "sell" the opportunity just as you would learn how to sell any product or service.

You need to be able to tell your story and share your vision in a compelling way. You also need to learn how to speak the language of the investment community. Making presentations and speeches in front of thousands is a regular part of my life, so I thought pitching to investors would be a piece of cake. Wrong. It was an entirely new ballgame. Fortunately, I participated in a venture capital "boot camp" for CEOs seeking equity investors. It was an intense six-to-eight-week training program, but it was well worth the investment of time and money. Without the great coaching and knowledge I gained from the program, I never would have stood a chance in front of investors. At the end of boot camp, the participating companies presented to a group of Silicon Valley venture capitalists. Frankly, I was a nervous wreck, but the hard work paid off; SBTV.com was selected as the best investment opportunity. It was an exciting moment for my partners and me.

Now, you're probably wondering what makes investment presentations so different from others. As the founder of your company, you could probably speak for hours about your business and how great your idea is. But if you get a face-to-face meeting with equity investors, you won't have more than 10 to 15 minutes to convince them that your business is worth their investment. So you have to understand what their hot buttons are and then focus on those elements. Here are some tips based on my experience in making VC presentations:

• *Identify your business.* Explain your business concept in the context of how it solves a market need. As I mentioned earlier, some experts refer to this as the "pain." What's the pain, or problem? How is your business the solution? Talk about the experience your business will deliver to the market and why this is important to your target customers.

• *Explain the big vision.* Because VCs are interested in high-growth companies, they want your take on the big picture. What is the big potential of your business—and why do you see it that way?

• *Pitch the market potential.* When I discussed business planning, I talked about understanding the size of your market. When you pitch to a VC, this is where the "no kidding around" rule applies. In Chapter 6, I talked about the size of the pet industry and its growth projections. For a VC, you need to be specific about how much of that market is going to be interested in your product or service, and why. Your numbers must be well thought out and defensible. In other words, be prepared to explain exactly how you made your calculations. Vague extrapolations are insufficient. Hard data is a must.

• *Describe your secret sauce.* What is really going to drive your success? Is it your team? Is it proprietary technology? Is it a new process that is more streamlined and cost-effective than others?

The same old way of doing business isn't going to capture the attention of a VC.

• *Provide the revenue model.* How is your business going to make money? For example, with ItsYourBiz.com, our business model was based on advertising. Therefore, we demonstrated how every visitor to our site created revenue for the company.

• *Present realistic financials.* In a VC presentation, financial projections are critical. While they should demonstrate impressive growth, they must also be realistic. In this economy, companies that project hockey-stick growth are most likely not living in the real world. By hockey-stick growth I mean revenues that go from nothing to hundreds of millions in a few short years. Remember, VCs analyze companies all the time. They can quickly size up any deal, so you want to make sure your financials are plausible.

• *Outline your use of funds.* Your presentation needs to describe how you're going to use the money you raise, and how those expenditures will drive revenue. Again, you'll need to be specific.

• *Name the price.* You are asking for an investment. How much money do you need? Will this be the only round of funding you expect to need, or will you need additional rounds to build your vision?

Chances are good that you'll make your presentation with the aid of PowerPoint. But don't use PowerPoint as a crutch, and don't make it too busy. Keep it simple and to the point. Try to limit the number of slides you use to between eight and ten. Make sure the last slide contains all your contact information. Practice your pre - sentation so that it sounds professional, but not memorized.

Venture capital firms don't roll out the red carpet for everyone. If you don't have the right connections, it is difficult to get in the door. Leverage your professional networks to identify people who may be involved in the VC world. While you can find a list of venture capital firms through the National Venture Capital Association, your chances of getting in without a warm introduction are slim to none. It's a tough game. And keep in mind that the venture capital process is time-consuming. It can take anywhere from six months to a couple of years to secure the funding you need.

- - -

As you have seen in this chapter, understanding your revenue model and demonstrating how you will make money are integral factors in raising funds to build your business. In the next chapter, we will discuss pricing and process for your business to help you execute on your business growth strategy.

CHAPTER 11

---

pricing and process

HOW MUCH SHOULD you charge for your product or service? In theory, you know you want to make a profit, so that means you need to charge more than it costs you to make and deliver your product or service. But in practice, it isn't as easy as it sounds to determine the right pricing structure for your business.

Finding the Perfect Price

Pricing a product is a little easier than pricing a service because there are hard costs associated with the production of the product, leaving fewer unknowns. But whether it's a product or a service, the basic equation is:

$$\text{cost} + \text{markup} = \text{retail price.}$$

Of course, your actual cost consists of more than just your out-of-pocket expenditures. That is, your cost includes both fixed and variable items. Your fixed costs are the items you buy that go into making the product. The variable costs include marketing, business overhead, salaries, travel, sales commissions, shipping, and so on. To determine the full cost of producing a product or service, you must allocate a percentage of the variable costs to each item you produce and add that to the fixed cost.

The appropriate markup for a product is fairly simple, based on what is generally accepted in your industry. Many retailers customarily use a markup of 100 percent. A wholesaler is going to use a lower markup. But, once again, that depends on the product and industry. It is more difficult to determine the appropriate markup for services. To get a general idea, check out what the competition is charging—the going rate for your type of service. As a rule of thumb, you don't want to be the most expensive, but you don't want to be the lowest-cost provider either.

In part, your markup is determined by how much profit you want to make; however, there is more to consider, such as what the market will bear—and this last factor is subjective. The market's receptiveness to your pricing depends on the value it places on the product or service. Some customers pay hundreds of dollars for a haircut, while others won't spend more than $20 or $30. Car fanatics often shell out hundreds of thousands of dollars for prestigious, high-end sports cars, and then there are people, like me, who really don't care what they drive. If you have no idea what is standard for your business, check the *Annual Statement Studies* published by the

Risk Management Association (RMA) to get averages. The information is also available online via the RMA website, www.rmahq.org.

Don't Sell Yourself Short

Often one of the big mistakes new business owners make is not charging enough for their services. Sometimes it's because they don't understand their cost structure, and sometimes it's because they are so desperate for the business that they're afraid to charge more. Regardless of the reason, charging too little is not a good idea. It will not bring you more business and it may actually drive business away.

If you believe your product or service offers customers great value, then trust that customers will pay for what they perceive is of value to them. Your challenge is to communicate the value you offer. Alternatively, if you charge bargain-basement prices, not only do you look desperate, but it implies that your product isn't valuable. If *you* don't value your business offering, why should anyone else?

Competing in the marketplace on price alone is a huge mistake. There is always someone out there who will be willing to provide the product or service for less than you can. That's particularly true if you are competing with major chains or retail discounters. You are almost never going to win at that game. They have more resources and can sustain a low profit margin, or even a loss, until they have put you out of business. Plus, once you establish low prices, it is difficult for customers to accept higher ones.

I learned this lesson early on. One of the services I sell is keynote speeches. When I first started speaking, I always underpriced myself. In fact, I sometimes accepted bookings for no fee and payment of expenses only, thinking that would bring in more engagements. Then I started talking with other speakers, and I asked them how they went about pricing their speaking services. Boy, was that ever a wake-up call! I realized that by trying to be flexible and open to opportunities, I was actually diluting my brand. So I established a fee structure and added a booking agent to my team. Now, I get more speaking engagements and earn a fee that is on par with others in my field.

Not All Sales Are Good Sales

Are you surprised that I would suggest such a thing? After all, you do need sales to build your business. But to build a sustainable company, there are times when less is more, and you need to recognize those times.

As I noted, many small businesses reduce their prices with the goal of generating more business. However, even if sales do increase, your company's profitability will end up suffering. In fact, even when gross revenues look good, it's possible that your company could reach a point where it is in a negative cash-flow position. (This can happen especially when your business is offered a new opportunity that drives it beyond what it's been doing with the overhead and markup you've established.)

All new sales opportunities must be considered carefully. Such situations are difficult to turn around, which is why not all sales are good sales. Before you forge ahead, you need to analyze your internal costs, including all your business overhead. Is there enough profit to absorb any changes or adjustments? Do you have the current staffing and resources to manage the new project without jeopardizing existing business?

Here's a real-life example. ABC Company bid on a large government contract to deliver a particular service without first doing a detailed and thorough analysis of the resources required. After winning the bid, it found that the additional internal resources and development needed to execute the contract turned what the owner thought would be a highly profitable project into one that barely broke even. Furthermore, because of the strain on the company's resources, other projects had to be delayed.

I'm sure you've heard the expression "Cash is king." This is true for any business, and no company can jeopardize its financial health by selling too much for too little. While it's hard to turn business away, you can be more successful by concentrating on the business opportunities that will be most profitable. And it's not always just about turning away new business. Some companies are choosing to fire their low-margin customers, and as a result are experiencing healthier bottom-line profits.

Every Business Needs Process

In addition to developing an appropriate pricing structure, you need to create the systems that will help your business run smoothly and efficiently. Systems provide sustainability for your company— whereby work can be replicated time and time again, with consistent results. Without the proper systems in place, your business will suffer from lower productivity and potentially serious mistakes, which can result in lost business and profits.

To create the right processes for your business, analyze all your operations. Review the work flow, including your own. Are there ways in which things could be managed more efficiently? Are certain activities being repeated unnecessarily? Do you follow the same course of action for every project, or are you constantly reinventing the wheel?

Once you get a handle on the best way to manage each of the various aspects of your business, document those processes. As your business grows and you add team members or new offerings, update your process guidelines. Even if there are only a couple of you working in the business, document how things get done. What would happen if you got sick or were hit by a bus? Documentation gives someone else the basic information they would need to manage your business.

When we were growing ItsYourBiz.com, one of my partners, who happened to be the architect of our technology platform, was diagnosed with stage-three melanoma. Suddenly, one of the key players of our team was missing, and unfortunately he hadn't written down all the means and methods—the keys to the kingdom. As with many entrepreneurs, the three of us kept much of the information about business operations in our heads. And that cost us—financially and in terms of lost opportunities. Fortunately, we managed to survive, but not all businesses are so lucky. Often the loss of a key player results in the actual demise of a business because proper documentation and systems haven't been established.

Leverage Technology for a Competitive Advantage

Technology is the driving force behind the surge in small-business start-ups. Technology levels the playing field and allows small businesses to do business anywhere in the world from anywhere they choose. As technology continues to advance, small companies are enjoying the benefits of increased productivity and profitability.

So every small-business owner needs to embrace technology in every aspect of the business, from things such as accounting and data management to marketing and sales support. If you aren't familiar with all the technology-based tools available for your business, then I recommend working with an IT consultant who can help you select appropriate hardware and software to fit your business needs.

• *Create a technology vision.* You'll need a technology plan for your business, and a professional consultant can help you develop that. A technology plan prevents you from making the mistake of jumping from one system or application to another, which isn't efficient and can be costly. A technology vision helps you make choices that will be appropriate for your business now, and will also grow with your business.

• *Buy the best fit.* Small-business owners can get caught up in the glitzy aspects of technologies, and as a result, they often buy more than they need. Purchasing the latest and greatest not only results in unused capacity, but it may also result in the technology not getting used at all because it is too complicated. So make a list of what your business needs are now, and what they are likely to be very soon, and make an investment in technology that satisfies those needs.

• *Establish a budget.* Just as with any other area of your business, you need to establish a budget for your technology. An IT professional can help you determine the appropriate amount you should allocate in order to meet your objectives. Without an established budget, you may wind up out of funds before you've been able to purchase everything you need.

• *Get training.* Technology isn't worth a dime if you don't use it. So invest in the proper training for you and your team. Often the vendor will offer to train you for no additional cost. Take advantage of this opportunity and carve the time out of your schedule so you can utilize your investment. Remember, the technology is there to help you become more productive and profitable.

An Office in the Palm of Your Hand

Mobile technology has taken the small-business world by storm. Because of smartphones, tablet computers, and iPads, entrepreneurs can stay connected and in control of nearly every aspect of their businesses from anywhere. It is a game changer.

A survey from Staples, the office supplies chain, found that small-business owners spent 60 percent more time holding their mobile devices than holding the hand of a significant other. Some may find this a little sad—letting smartphones and mobile devices permeate every minute of our day. But on the other hand, for small businesses that are embracing the new technology, it brings more balance to the owners' lives. The smartphone can be viewed as a handheld virtual office. So, if you want to duck out of the office to head over to your child's soccer game, you can do it. It is the ultimate multitasking tool.

Smartphones are basically small computers, and they are changing the way many small businesses do business. A smartphone can do most anything your computer can do. (Of course, if you're over a certain age, reading glasses may be necessary, but nonetheless, the capability is there.) But if you aren't up to speed on everything your smartphone can do, let me hit some of the highlights. All of these options can help you run your business smarter, faster, and better.

• *Bookkeeping.* There are applications that allow businesses to track income and expenses and sync everything in real time with their accounting software programs. This increases productivity and accuracy. Because I travel a lot, I use my smartphone for keeping track of expenses on the road. As a result, I don't forget to write things down or submit expense reports. Without a doubt, it has saved me a significant amount of money.

• *Credit card processing.* You can take credit card payments via your smartphone now. So if you're selling out in the field, it's a quicker and easier way of processing payments.

• *Inventory and time management.* Real-time inventory management tools provide a method for small businesses to track their inventory much like a large company, leveling the playing field. For service companies that bill by the hour, there are time-tracking tools—which means no more paper time sheets.

• *Marketing.* More companies are using mobile text messaging for marketing. Incorporating text numbers into any television, radio, or print ads makes it easier for customers to make quick purchases. And let's not forget social media. The smartphone connects you to all social media applications so you can manage your marketing activities from anywhere. According to Facebook, more than 200 million users access its site through mobile devices. What's more, those who use social media on the go are more active on the sites than nonmobile users. Personally, I manage everything from my phone, so when people say they don't have time to utilize this marketing tool, I simply direct them to their smartphones.

The possibilities for newer and better productivity and management tools are endless. So, could the smartphone be the answer to work/life balance? I can't say for sure, but it does help a small-business owner manage operations more easily. It certainly helps when your entire office is in the palm of your hand. Bottom line: As a small-business owner, consider investing some time in educating yourself about the mobile applications that can help you grow your business.

CHAPTER 12

words of wisdom from the trenches

Making a decision to start a company is the easiest decision to make. It is sustaining the business for four years and doing things like making payroll, getting legal representation, trademark issues, those are the harder things.

—David Schenberg, CEO and
cofounder of BusyEvent

EVERY BUSINESS needs a key differentiator. My differentiator is my real-world experience. I don't dole out advice solely based on writing and reporting about entrepreneurs. Instead, I have lived every aspect of what you are going through. So this chapter is devoted to sharing some thoughts that don't fit into any of the general business categories. By sharing these final words of wisdom from the trenches, I hope I can help you successfully navigate the challenges that are unique to new and growing business owners.

Don't Chase Your Tail

In Chapter 9, I mentioned that my dog, Maxwell, quietly lies at my feet when I work at my home office. Because Maxwell is still very young, he loves to play. He has more toys and treats than you can imagine, but one of his favorite things to do is chase his tail. He runs in a circle at manic speed until he ultimately collapses, never achieving his goal, if he even knows what his goal is. That doesn't stop him, however, from trying again later.

It's perfectly acceptable for a puppy to chase his tail. After all, he's a dog and that's what dogs do. But when you're working to build a successful business, it's not so cute to spend time, energy, and resources chasing your tail. You'll end up going nowhere, and before you know it, you'll likely get burned out because you're not accomplishing anything.

So as you're building your business, take introspective looks at yourself periodically. Are you chasing your tail? On how many days have you had lots of activity going on, but at the end of the day, you've accomplished nothing to move your business forward? I see it all the time. People "make busy." They create lots of commotion, and they talk a good game, but their business is going nowhere.

Keep Moving Forward

Here are a few surefire tips to help you grow your business—and keep you from chasing your tail:

• *Keep your eye on the ball.* When you start a business, money is always tight. Attractive opportunities may present themselves as quick ways to bring in revenue, but they may be complete departures from your core business strategy. Before you decide to go for one, stop and think about the ramifications of your decision. How much of a distraction will this be?

One of the most common reasons small businesses fail is that they take on projects or products that are completely unrelated to their business strategy, and as a result, the original business suffers. It's impossible to be all things to all people. Stay focused on your core business.

• *Set milestones.* Establish deadlines and/or milestones for yourself. Without established measurements, days, weeks, and months can pass while you talk, talk, talk about what you're going to do— but never get around to doing it. You may not meet every one of your goals in the time frame you estimated, but at least you'll be continually focused on moving forward.

• *Take action every day.* Never let a day go by in which you haven't done at least one activity to help you reach your business goals. Business success requires discipline—the discipline to consistently practice those things that are instrumental for your success. Attending a networking event or making a sales call only occasionally won't help you generate the number of new business opportunities you'll need. You know better than anyone else the actions that will be necessary to grow your business. Make sure you practice them every day.

Listen to Your Instincts

I've said numerous times in this book that it is impossible for you to know everything you need to know about building your business. Now, I add a caveat: Asking for advice and guidance to help you run your business is always a smart idea; however, blindly following that advice without listening to your own instincts can get you into trouble. When you're worried and stressed about keeping your business going, it's tempting to rely on someone else's strategy.

Before you make that mistake, consider this. Most cars today have GPS systems. My new iPhone has one. The taxis in New York City have them. And if you don't have one you can access on the go, you can get directions from online mapping sites. It's simple. Type in where you want to go and follow the directions to your desired destination. So why can't you get directions and follow them in your business? Seems simple.

Well, what happens if your GPS is wrong? What happens if the business directions you get are wrong for your business? My husband and I were traveling in the Southern United States on a media tour for my last book, *The Girls' Guide to Building a Million-Dollar Business*. As we were driving back to our home in St. Louis, we decided to stop in Tunica, Mississippi. (For those of you who don't know, Tunica is just south of Memphis, Tennessee, and it is in what was once the poorest county in the United States. Today, more than 10 million visitors make their way to Tunica, which is now considered the casino capital of the South.)

Since we didn't have a clue about how to get to Tunica from where we were, we turned to the car's GPS system. We identified our starting location and selected a visitor site in Tunica as our destination. We were on our way. Periodically, our electronic guide would tell us where to turn, as well as inform us on how far it was to our destination. Thirty minutes into our journey, Lola (the name we gave our electronic guide) had us taking desolate two-lane roads. Where was Lola taking us? Even though we were somewhat skeptical, we let Lola continue to dictate our path. It was the gravel and dirt road that served as our wake-up call. My husband flagged down a very nice man and his wife in a pickup, who told us the road we were on led to the water's edge, and Tunica was across the river; there was no way to get across the river unless we had an amphibious vehicle. We had no choice but to turn around and retrace our route in order to get back on the right road to Tunica.

My point is, if we had allowed our instincts to guide us when things starting looking odd, we wouldn't have gone more than an hour out of our way. But Lola had sold us a bill of goods. In business, if we'd made the same mistake, we might have been all washed up.

So remember to ask yourself, *"Does it make sense to follow the gravel and dirt road to a well-known tourist site?"* Here's to staying dry and to making your business a success.

Manage Growth Wisely

The recent economic downturn has slowed growth for many companies. Most experts believe the days of triple-digit annual growth rates are gone. But there is nothing that says you need to sprint to the finish line. In fact, growing a business can be better analogized to running a marathon. *Controlled growth* can be a smart business strategy.

Overextending yourself and your resources by taking on too much too fast can kill your business. Rapid expansion can cause you to lose focus, drain your finances, and ultimately break the system. You don't want your company to be a flash in the pan. You want its star rising and shining brightly for a long time.

It's not uncommon for early-stage businesses to find themselves in a situation whereby they can't keep pace with their growth. Managing growth in a healthy way is critical for survival. That means you should know what your business capacity is at any given time and how much further you can stretch without risking your financial solvency. Some expansion opportunities may have to be tabled for the time being—at least until you're confident you have sufficient resources.

In my business, we look at growth initiatives as "above the line" and "below the line." Recognizing that we have the resources to tackle only a certain number of new projects at a time, we prioritize them. Those that are above the line become our focus and those below the line are put on hold. The list may change, depending on a variety of circumstances, but it is a good discipline that keeps us focused on the right growth strategies.

Fast-growth companies often take shortcuts and hold things together with Band-Aids and duct tape. It reminds me of a hamster running on one of those little wheels—they go faster and faster but get nowhere. Once your business operations falter, it's difficult to regain your momentum. So, as you grow your business, make sure you can substantiate the growth and continue to fulfill customer or client expectations.

When you develop your growth plans, be as realistic as possible about how much you'll truly be able to achieve. Take a look at your resources and don't overextend. Not only will it be stressful for you, but the chances are you'll lose customers or clients in the process. Remember, there is no such thing as an overnight success.

Collaborative Opportunities Can Help You Grow

In today's competitive business world, collaboration is integral to success. It's tough to survive as an island. As a result, many businesses are growing their firms by creating strategic alliances. These alliances allow you to take on bigger contracts, offer more services, or cover larger geographic territories. They also provide a way to develop best practices: Two heads are better than one; collaborative brainpower is a significant asset.

How do you find companies with whom to align? You probably already know people in your industry or a related industry who could partner with you to go after a major contract opportunity. If not, check with your industry association to see whether it has a database you could access for this type of business match-making. Some associations have newsletters in which businesses can advertise for alliance partners. Current clients can also be a good resource. Ask who they might recommend.

And don't forget social media. The connections I've made with people via social media have led to business opportunities. Remember, social media is networking cyber-charged so use it as a resource tool for any occasion where networking would be advantageous.

Expect the Unexpected

It seems every time I turn on the news, there is a natural disaster being reported somewhere in the world. The scenes of suffering and devastation are heartbreaking. This sure makes you realize how vulnerable we all are. Disaster can strike anytime, anywhere, demolishing our homes, ruining our businesses, and stealing away friends and family members. Yet, few of us take the necessary steps to prepare ourselves for when a disaster hits. Particularly, small businesses.

I've found that it's only when disaster strikes that small businesses focus on learning more about disaster preparedness and risk management. Then, when things calm down and the headlines move on to other stories, entrepreneurs revert to business as usual. The sense of urgency is gone.

What would you do if you faced a disaster? Are you prepared? Your business could be hit tomorrow with something unexpected that interferes with your ability to conduct business operations. And it doesn't have to be a major natural disaster to be devastating. What if the sprinkler system goes off in your building, or a major pipe breaks, destroying all electronic systems, customer files, and inventory? Think about what you'd do if construction workers nearby cut water mains and electrical lines causing outages for several days. Could you continue your business operations?

It is impossible to prevent disasters from striking your company, but you can take action in advance to limit the impact your business sustains. Here are a few suggestions:

- *Make a list of business essentials.* Determine which staff, materials, procedures, and equipment are absolutely necessary to keep your business operating.

- *Create a contact list.* Make sure you have a list of your suppliers, customers, and other business resources—and make sure it's also available at an off-site location.

- *Maintain document storage.* Keep duplicate files of all critical business documents, or store them virtually, at a separate location.

- *Review your insurance coverage.* Be sure it is up-to-date and covers all your assets.

- *Secure emergency supplies.* Have on hand a battery-operated radio and extra batteries, water, food, first-aid supplies, etc.

You can also find guidelines for personal and business risk management on the website Ready.gov.

Learn to Manage Your Stress

The stress of growing your business can take its toll. That's why it's important to take care of *you*. Stress is the number-one cause of illness in our country. Learning how to manage your stress level is not only smart, it's also critically important for your business success. When you are stressed or not feeling well, your motivation level drops. Your judgment and decision making can become impaired. Certainly, emotions can quickly escalate, resulting in irrational behavior or fits of anger.

Be realistic about what you can expect of yourself and don't overcommit. Learn to say "no" and really mean it. Before you say "yes" to something, make sure it would be the most appropriate use of your time and resources. Remember, you can't change the number of hours in a day—but you can manage your time and plan ahead to have your schedule accommodate time to focus on your personal well-being. If you don't, you'll burn out, and so will your business.

Try scheduling some time during the week that is just for you, and do something you really enjoy. For example, a woman recently told me she leaves her office once a week to take a piano lesson. The lesson and her practice time throughout the week force her to think about something entirely different from her business challenges. As a result, it helps her feel refreshed and more creative.

Another friend related a story from when she was growing her salon and spa business. She was working 24/7. One evening when she came home, her husband asked for a divorce. Shocked, she asked him why. He explained that she was never home, and that when she was with him, she was really thinking about the business. Fortunately, this served as a wake-up call for my friend, and she was able to both salvage her marriage and continue to build her business.

Exercise, eating right, socializing with family and friends—all of these things are easily forgotten when you are struggling to build a business. But they are important for your health and well-being. Discover what works best for you, and make a commitment to yourself and your business that taking care of you is as important as caring for and nurturing the growth of your business.

Enjoy the journey!

resources for start-ups and expanding businesses

THE CHALLENGE OF writing a book like this is getting to an endpoint. There is so much to say on the subject of starting and growing your own business. But assuming I even could address every possible topic and answer every likely question, you'd never be able to lift the book. Therefore, I leave you with a list of some great resources that can help you accelerate your business's growth. (To provide you with the most accurate information, the text in these entries is borrowed from the organizations' websites.) This list is not all-encompassing by any means; but they are some of my favorite resources and I hope you'll find them useful.

Associations and Organizations that Foster Small Business

Government Agencies

Small Business Administration (SBA). The SBA was created in 1953 as an independent agency of the federal government to aid, counsel, assist, and protect the interests of small-business concerns, to preserve free competitive enterprise, and to maintain and strengthen the overall economy of our nation. The SBA helps Americans start, build, and grow businesses. Through an extensive network of field offices and partnerships with public and private organizations, the SBA delivers its services to people throughout the United States, Puerto Rico, the U.S. Virgin Islands, and Guam. Contact: www.sba.gov.

SBA Online Women's Business Center. This group assists *women* in achieving their dreams of starting a business, regardless of social or financial disadvantage, race, ethnicity, or business background. Contact: www.onlinewbc.gov.

Small Business Development Centers (SBDCs). The federal government's Small Business Development Centers provide management assistance to current and prospective small-business owners. They offer one-stop assistance to individuals and small businesses by providing information and guidance in central and easily accessible branch locations. Contact: www.sba.gov/sbdc.

National Women's Business Council (NWBC). The National Women's Business Council is a bipartisan federal advisory council created to serve as an independent source of advice and policy recommendations to the president, Congress, and the U.S. Small Business

Administration on economic issues of importance to women business owners. The Council's mission is to promote bold initiatives, policies, and programs designed to support women's business enterprises at all stages of development in public and private sector marketplaces—from start-up to success to significance. Contact: www. nwbc.gov.

Educational and Advocacy Business Organizations

American Management Association (AMA). A world leader in talent development, advancing the skills of individuals to drive business success, the AMA's approach is to improve performance by combining experiential learning—learning through doing—with opportunities for ongoing professional growth at every step of one's career journey. The AMA supports the goals of individuals and organizations through a complete range of products and services, including classroom and live online seminars, webcasts, webinars, podcasts, conferences, corporate and government solutions, business books, and research. Organizations worldwide, including the majority of the Fortune 500, turn to AMA as their trusted partner in professional development and draw upon its experience to enhance skills, abilities, and knowledge with noticeable results from day one. Contact: www.amanet.org.

Entrepreneurs' Organization (EO). This is a dynamic global network of more than 7,000 business owners in nearly 40 countries. Founded in 1987 by a group of young entrepreneurs, EO is the catalyst that enables entrepreneurs to learn from each other, leading to greater business success and an enriched personal life. EOtv, the EO's weekly webcast, provides rich business learning from entrepreneurs such as Gene Simmons (KISS), Rachael Ray, and Tony Hsieh (Zappos.com). In partnership with Mercedes-Benz Financial, the EO also operates the Global Student Entrepreneur

Awards program, the premier award for undergraduate students who own and operate businesses while attending a college or university; as well as the Accelerator Program, a series of quarterly, high-impact learning events that provide business owners with the tools, knowledge, and skills to grow their businesses to more than $1 million in annual revenue. Contact: www.eonetwork.org.

Ewing Marion Kauffman Foundation. The Foundation's vision is to foster a society of economically independent individuals who are engaged citizens, contributing to the improvement of their communities. It focuses grant making and operations on two areas: advancing entrepreneurship and improving the education of children and youth—offering four programmatic areas: Entrepreneurship, Advancing Innovation, Education, and Research and Policy. Contact: www.kauffman.org.

Freelancers Union. Freelancers Union and its members are building a new support system to help the growing independent workforce thrive. The organization's mission is to promote the interests of independent workers through advocacy, education, and service. Contact: www.freelancersunion.org.

National Association for the Self-Employed (NASE). This is the nation's leading resource for the self-employed and microbusinesses, providing a broad range of benefits and support to help the smallest businesses succeed. Contact: www.nase.org.

National Business Incubation Association (NBIA). The world's leading organization advancing business incubation and entrepreneurship, this organization each year provides thousands of professionals with information, education, advocacy, and networking resources to bring excellence to the process of assisting early-stage companies. An elected, voting board of directors representing the world's leading incubators governs the association. Contact: www.nbia.org.

National Federation of Independent Businesses (NFIB). A leading advocacy organization representing small and independent businesses, this nonprofit, nonpartisan organization founded in 1943 represents the consensus views of its members in Washington and all 50 state capitals. NFIB's mission is to promote and protect the rights of its members to own, operate, and grow their businesses. NFIB also gives its members a power in the marketplace. Contact: www.nfib.org.

National Inventor Fraud Center (NIFC). The organization's goal is to provide information to consumers about invention-promotion companies and how people can market their ideas. Inventors often do not realize that some invention marketing companies charge thousands of dollars, yet have success rates of 0.00 percent. The goal of the NIFC is to educate and help inventors make the right decisions. Contact: www.inventorfraud.com.

National Small Business Association (NSBA). A national nonprofit membership organization founded in 1937, this group represents America's small-business companies and entrepreneurs. Reaching more than 150,000 small businesses, NSBA is the first and oldest national small-business advocacy organization in the United States. Contact: www.nsba.biz.

Service Corps of Retired Executives (SCORE). A resource partner with the SBA, SCORE is a nonprofit association dedicated to educating entrepreneurs and helping small businesses start, grow, and succeed nationwide. SCORE's valuable network of more than 13,000 knowledgeable and experienced volunteers offers small-business entrepreneurs confidential business counseling services at no charge. Its volunteers represent more than 270,000 years of experience across 62 industries. SCORE also provides local workshops and events throughout the country to connect small-business owners with the people and information they need to start, grow, and maintain their businesses, as well as online workshops available 24/7. Contact: www.score.org.

United Inventors Association. Since 1990, the UIA is the national 501(c) nonprofit dedicated to inventor education and support. Its mission is to provide reliable information to inventors, as well as certification to groups and inventor-friendly firms that agree to comply with rigorous professional and ethical standards. Contact: www.uiausa.org.

Organizations That Promote Women-Owned Businesses and Networking

Association of Women's Business Centers (AWBC). The AWBC develops and strengthens a global network of women's business centers to advance the growth and success of women business owners. The vision of AWBC is a world where economic justice, wealth, and well-being are realized through the collective leadership and power of successful entrepreneurial women. Contact: www.awbc.biz.

Athena International. This group pairs woman-owned businesses with a group of local mentors who serve as a panel of advisers. Advisers work with the business owner on her business for one year at no charge. Contact: www.AthenaInternational.org.

Ladies Who Launch (LWL). This is a group that provides content and community to help women start and expand their businesses and creative ventures. Through their events, email newsletter, website, and in-person incubator programs, Ladies Who Launch provides a venue for motivated women to exchange products and services, ideas, and strategic relationships. Contact: www.ladies wholaunch.com.

National Association of Women Business Owners (NAWBO). Since 1975, NAWBO has helped women evolve their businesses by sharing resources and providing a single voice to shape economic and public policy. NAWBO is the only dues-based national organization representing the interests of all women entrepreneurs across all industries. Contact: www.nawbo.org.

Women Impacting Public Policy (WIPP). This is a national bipartisan public policy organization that advocates for and on behalf of women-owned businesses and educates women business owners on economic policy and current legislative initiatives that impact business health and growth. Contact: www.wipp.org.

Women's Business Enterprise National Council (WBENC). Founded in 1997, WBENC is the nation's leading advocate of women-owned businesses as suppliers to America's corporations. It also is the largest third-party certifier of businesses owned and operated by women in the United States. WBENC works to foster diversity in the world of commerce with programs and policies designed to expand opportunities and eliminate barriers in the marketplace for women business owners. Contact: www.wbenc.org.

Women's Leadership Exchange (WLE). Founded by and for successful businesswomen, WLE's mission is to provide the knowledge, tools, and connections that women need to be successful in their own businesses, the corporate world, and the not-for-profit environment. WLE offers a resource-packed website, teleconferences, an e-newsletter, local presentations, and a facilitated connection program. Contact: www.womensleadershipexchange.com.

■ ■ ■

In addition to these women's general membership organizations, you'll find other groups providing more specific services for women in other categories in this appendix.

Organizations That Foster Minority-Owned Small Businesses

National Association of Minority Contractors (NAMC). This is a non-profit trade association established in 1969 to address the needs and concerns of minority contractors. While membership is open to people of all races and ethnic backgrounds, the organization's mandate, "Building Bridges—Crossing Barriers," focuses on construction-industry concerns common to African Americans, Asian Americans, Hispanic Americans, and Native Americans. Contact: www.namc national.org.

National Black Chamber of Commerce. Dedicated to economically empowering and sustaining African American communities through entrepreneurship and capitalistic activity within the United States, this group reaches more than 100,000 black-owned businesses. Contact: www.nationalbcc.org.

National Minority Supplier Development Council (NMSDC). A direct link between corporate America and minority-owned businesses, the NMSDC provides increased procurement and business opportunities for minority businesses of all sizes. Regional councils certify and match more than 16,000 minority-owned businesses (Asian, black, Hispanic, and Native American) with member corporations that want to purchase goods and services. Contact: www.nmsdc.org.

U.S. Hispanic Chamber of Commerce (USHCC). The USHCC works to bring the concerns of the nation's almost three million Hispanic-owned businesses to the forefront of the national economic agenda. Through its network of more than 200 local Hispanic Chambers of Commerce and Hispanic business organizations, the USHCC effectively communicates the needs and potential of Hispanic enterprise to the public and private sector. This includes providing technical assistance to Hispanic business associations and entrepreneurs. Contact: www.ushcc.com.

Specialty Organizations and Associations

Alliance for Virtual Businesses™ *(A4VB)*. Established in 2003, this organization's primary mission includes promoting the growth of free enterprise between virtual assistants, entrepreneurs, small businesses, corporations, associations, and other business entities. Business owners can learn about the time- and cost-saving advantages of working with a virtual assistant. The A4VB also provides training, education, mentoring, and coaching for virtual assistants. Contact: www.allianceforvirtualbiz.com.

Direct Marketing Association (DMA). The DMA is the leading global trade association of businesses and nonprofit organizations using and supporting multichannel direct marketing tools and techniques. The DMA advocates industry standards for responsible marketing both online and offline, promotes relevance as the key to reaching consumers with desirable offers, and provides cutting-edge research, education, and networking opportunities to improve results throughout the end-to-end direct marketing process. Contact: www.the-dma.org.

Direct Selling Association (DSA). The DSA is the national trade association of the leading firms that manufacture and distribute goods and services sold directly to consumers. DSA's services are designed to enable member companies to make better-informed and smarter operating decisions. Contact: www.dsa.org.

International Franchise Association (IFA). The oldest and largest franchising trade group, the IFA helps educate prospective franchise investors so they are equipped to handle the challenges of becoming small-business entrepreneurs. The IFA website provides detailed information for more than 1,100 franchises; a broad list of subject-matter experts; and a comprehensive library of franchising information, ranging from basic "how-to's" to advanced regulatory and legal information. Contact: www.franchise.org.

Mom Invented. This organization helps women start businesses and develop products and inventions with inventing advice, inspirational inventing help, and business advice. Contact: www.mominventors.com.

National Association of Manufacturers (NAM). The nation's largest industrial trade association, NAM is a strong voice for the American manufacturing community, representing manufacturers large and small in every industrial sector and in all 50 states. It is the leading advocate for government policies that reduce the cost of production and break down barriers to exports. Its staff of policy experts provides information on the key issues affecting the manufacturer's business and bottom line: from healthcare reform and labor relations, to energy and the environment, to trade policy and taxes. Contact: www.nam.org.

National Restaurant Association (NRA). Since 1919, the NRA has been the restaurant industry's leading association. Representing more than 380,000 restaurants, suppliers, educators, and nonprofits, the NRA aims to help members build customer loyalty, find financial success, and provide rewarding careers in foodservice. Contact: www.restaurant.org.

Small Business Exporters Association (SBEA). The SBEA is a nonpartisan, nonprofit industry association dedicated to the creation and growth of small and midsize U.S. business exporters. (It is also the international trade arm of the National Small Business Association.) In addition to advocating on behalf of small-business exporters, it provides members with networking opportunities and cost-saving tools. Contact: www.sbea.org.

Organizations That Represent or Offer Financial Assistance

ACCION USA. A leader in U.S. microfinance, ACCION USA is committed to bringing affordable small-business loans to microentrepreneurs. ACCION USA has provided over $119 million in over 19,000 microloans for over 9,000 small-business owners since its inception in 1991. It offers business loans of up to $50,000 and financial education throughout the United States. ACCION USA specializes in working with small-business owners who cannot borrow from a bank due to business type, a short length of time in business, or an insufficient credit history. Contact: www.accionusa.org.

Astia. Founded in 1999 in Silicon Valley, this global, not-for-profit organization is a community of more than 1,000 experts committed to building women leaders and accelerating the funding and growth of the companies they lead. Astia connects entrepreneurs to investors, industry leaders, advisers, and service providers, with the aim of delivering results by facilitating access to the proven pathways to success. Contact: www.astia.org.

Count Me In. This group champions the cause for women's economic independence by providing access to business loans, consultation, and education. The first online microlender, Count Me In uses a unique, women-friendly credit scoring system to make loans of $500 to $10,000 available to women across the United States who have nowhere else to turn for that all-important first business loan. The organization provides access to networks that expand contacts, markets, skills, and confidence. Contact: www.countmein.org.

Golden Seeds. Committed to empowering women financially, Golden Seeds is a network of angel investors dedicated to investing in early-stage companies founded and/or led by women. With locations in New York, Boston, Philadelphia, and San Francisco, it provides entrepreneurs with strategic business advice as well as access to funding and the tools to enable them to grow into multimillion-dollar businesses. Contact: www.goldenseeds.com.

Kiva. This is a nonprofit organization with a mission to connect people through lending to alleviate poverty. Leveraging the Internet and a worldwide network of microfinance institutions, Kiva lets individuals lend funding-worthy businesses as little as $25 to help create opportunity for entrepreneurs around the world. Contact: www.kiva.org.

National Association of Small Business Investment Companies (NASBIC). The NASBIC coordinates and promotes the activities of hundreds of small-business investment companies (SBIC) nationwide. SBICs are privately capitalized, owned, and managed investment firms licensed by the SBA that provide equity capital, long-term financing, and management assistance to small businesses. The SBIC program emphasizes investment in the small growth firms that generate jobs. Contact: www.nasbic.org.

Springboard Enterprises. Venture-catalyst Springboard Enterprises is a national nonprofit organization where entrepreneurs, investors, and industry experts converge to build great women-led businesses. Its programs educate, source, showcase, and support women entrepreneurs seeking equity capital to grow their companies. Contact www.springboardenterprises.com.

ItsYourBiz.com (IYB). IYB is a news and information website focused exclusively on small business. It broadcasts a daily video small-business news brief called "Today in Small Biz" to keep viewers apprised of hot topics. The site also features "how-to" information to help entrepreneurs start and grow their businesses, along with inspirational success stories. Viewers will find some of the nation's best experts to guide them to small-business success. Contact: www.itsyourbiz.com.

INDEX

ABOUT THE AUTHORS

Susan Wilson Solovic is a woman of many talents. She's an award-winning entrepreneur, a CEO, and a journalist, bestselling author, multimedia personality, and attorney. But behind every achievement, Solovic embodies ideas that make her universally—and intimately—relatable to all entrepreneurs: hard work, fortitude, and persistence. She is a rare commodity in a world of quick and incredible viral fame: She is what she preaches.

Raised in rural Missouri by entrepreneurial parents, Solovic learned early on the value and meaning of becoming one's own boss. At the age of 15, while most adolescents are preoccupied with growing up, Solovic had already started her own business giving baton-twirling lessons. Since then, Solovic's journey has taken her a long way from her twirling start, yet she has never lost grasp of those indelible early years. She would go on to be the first in her family to graduate from law school—made possible by working full-time. But later on, feeling that law was not her ultimate calling, Solovic tapped into her entrepreneurial spirit by building a company from the ground up. As the CEO and cofounder of ItsYourBiz.com (formerly SBTV.com), Solovic led the company from a concept to a multimillion-dollar, award-winning enterprise. In 2006, Solovic accepted the Stevie Award on behalf of ItsYourBiz.com for the Most Innovative Company under 100 employees; that same year, ItsYourBiz.com was voted the Best Investment Opportunity presenting to a Venture Forum event in the Silicon Valley.

Solovic is a self-proclaimed overachiever, and her litany of achievements does not end there. She is also a sought-after keynote speaker, as well as a small-business contributor for ABC News. She appears frequently on MSBNC, Fox Business News, Good Day New York, WABC, WCBS, and many other stations across the country. In 2011, Solovic launched a nationally syndicated radio show, *It's Your Biz with Susan Solovic*, during which she invites leading entrepreneurial experts from across the country to share their unique perspectives on the world of small business. In conjunction with PBS, she created a feature program called *Reinvent Yourself Now: Become Self-Reliant in an Unpredictable World*. In addition to television and radio appearances, Solovic is a featured blogger on numerous sites, including Huffington Post, AllBusiness.com, ConstantContact, WSJ.com, U.S. Small Business Administration, and Fast Company.

Solovic has written three bestselling books: *The Girls' Guide to Power and Success; Reinvent Your Career: Attain the Success You Desire and Deserve;* and *The Girls' Guide to Building a Million-Dollar Business.* As a fervent activist for women entrepreneurs, she is a Vice President of the Board of Directors of WIPP, Women Impacting Public Policy. In 2009, Solovic received the Institute for Women's Entrepreneurship Leader of Distinction Award, and in 2008 she was the first recipient of AT&T's Innovator of the Year Award for being a pioneer in a new industry. WIPP honored Solovic with the President's Award in 2007, the organization's most prestigious recognition.

Apart from her professional achievements, Solovic also currently serves on the advisory board for the John Cook School of

Business Entrepreneurial Studies at Saint Louis University, one of the top-rated entrepreneurial schools in the United States. Previously, Solovic served on the National Women's Business Council, which counsels the President, Congress, and the SBA on issues impacting women business owners. She is also a past member of the Women's Leadership Board at Harvard University. And all the while she still finds time for hobbies. Solovic is an avid cook and pianist, and believes in living a healthy lifestyle. She has a passion for meeting and learning about new people and making a positive impact on their lives—this is her raison d'être. Having reinvented herself time and time again, while still holding on to core principles, she is an archetype of the entrepreneurial spirit that affords her a unique vantage point from which to share information and insight with business owners around the world.

You can contact Susan at info@itsyourbiz.com or www. ItsYourBiz.com.

■　■　■

Ellen R. Kadin is Executive Editor at AMACOM Books and a part-time writer. Kadin launched her glamorous publishing career updating a perennial bestseller—the *ASME Boiler and Pressure Vessel Code*. A marketing-oriented editor, she has since brought to life hundreds of successful books in a wide range of business, professional, and general-interest subject areas, specializing in business books.

Kadin was a contributor to Paul B. Brown's otherwise splendid book, *Publishing Confidential: The Insider's Guide to What It Really Takes to Land a Nonfiction Book Deal*. Rumors that she participates wantonly in each book she publishes are unfounded.

Ms. Kadin lives in New York City, currently spending too much time contemplating whether José Reyes will still be the Mets shortstop at the time of this book's publication.